Room for thought

A collection of poems written by

Joan Hankey

Chaldea Publishers

First edition

All Rights Reserved

Printed and bound in Great Britain
by Shelleys The Printers Ltd.
Sherborne, Dorset.

Designed by Robson Dowry

ISBN 978-0-9927647-0-8

▲

Published by Chaldea Publishers
Copyright © Chaldea Publishers

This book is dedicated:
To my Beloved Family

Do not be sad when I have gone
Just dry your tears and carry on
Rejoice that I have left a space
For someone else to take my place

I've lived my time and played my part
You know I'm there within your heart
But time moves on as we all know
And time has come for me to go

Time for me to meet my mate
He will be waiting at the gate
Eternally as we have planned
He will be there to take my hand

I have the faith and do believe
So please my children do not grieve
Your Guardian Angel at your side
Will give you strength and be your guide

The moon will be our meeting place
Look up at it and see my face
I will be smiling down on you
And showering love on all you do
I thank you All for your love and care
I know you'll cope when I'm not there.

Night Night. God Bless, Mum and Nan xx

Prologue

The words on these pages
Should not make you feel bad
They should point out some lessons
That I never had

They should make you think wisely
Not to make that mistake
And consider more carefully
Which road you should take

You may feel obliged
To take note from your peers
If you follow their path
It could all end in tears

But don't close your mind
When you're offered advice
Or follow a path
Because you think it sounds nice

Just weigh up all options
And then make your choice
Be certain to listen
To your inner voice

Your own intuition
Can rarely be wrong
It protects you and guides you
And makes you feel strong

But sometimes you know
You will make a mistake
It's part of the process
With each chance you take

You will take some knocks
As you follow your course
But the blow is much softer
When the decision was yours

Just dust yourself off
And keep your will strong
And bask in the glory
When success comes along

You will grow slightly stronger
When each lesson is learned
And you're safe in the knowledge
That you've got what you've earned.

Contents

4.	Do You Believe?
6.	Beloved
7.	Your Photo
8.	Through All Eternity
10.	The Curtain Call
12.	Who Am I
13.	Five Years On
14.	Vision or Dream
17.	Food for Thought
20.	My Little Mate
21.	The Power of Pure Thought
22.	The Cost of Change (Concrete Jungle)
24.	With Hindsight
26.	Don't
27.	When Can We
28.	A Walk in the Park
29.	What is Love?
30.	Life Continues on
31.	Wholeness
32.	Children
36.	Friends
37.	Deeds
38.	Life
40.	Into the Depth
42.	Think Twice
43.	Cosmic Twin
46.	Growing Up
49.	War Child
53.	Single Parent
54.	Family Tree
57.	The Headless Chicken
58.	Young Lives Lost
60.	No Pockets in a Shroud
62.	The Wind

65.	Unity
66.	Poetry Society
68.	Angels
70.	Old Friend
72.	When I was a Child
74.	The Wretched Child
77.	Fishing with Dad
79.	Over the Rainbow
82.	Children's Minds
83.	A Whim
84.	A Wise Man Watcheth
86.	The Girl on the Swing
88.	My Friend the Wind
90.	A Grandmother's Sorrow
91.	The Hanger On
92.	Who am I
93.	Do You Ever
94.	Open up your Mind
95.	A Sound Direction
96.	Air Raid
100.	Our Die is Cast
102.	The Cost of War
105.	Honour the Fallen
107.	The Lonely Soul
108.	Just the Mist
111.	The Queen
112.	Warm and Cosy
113.	Moving On
114.	Soul Mate
116.	Tomorrow
120.	A Poem for Rita
122.	A Soldier's Child
124.	An Imprint
125.	Quick Quote

126	Remembrance Day (Eleven Eleven)
127	Soul Mates
128	The Hankey Clan
129	The Garden
130	Teenagers
132	Old Oak Tree
134	Child of Light
135	The General
135	The Headless Man
136	This Little Book
137	My Little Book
138	Quick Quote
139	The Star
142	The Witch
145	The Comforter
146	Autumn Wind
148	A Focus Point
150	Love or Lust
151	Maundy Thursday
152	A Tramp
156	The Portrait
158	Young Tramp
159	Seven Candles
160	Reflection
162	Vicar Vicar

Do You Believe?

Do you believe
there's life above the Earth
or life below
this land's expansionary girth

Do you ever wonder
What that life could be
Like our life on Earth
Or that below the sea

Or could it simply be
A form of spirit and pure light
That can take on any form
For our mind's eye to delight

It may not always please us
Sometimes fear can turn to fright
It depends upon our state of mind
when we go to bed at night

Do you believe
The tales aforetime told
Of God's creation
Light and darkness, heat and cold

You can't deny the things
That stare you in the face
Nor explain why some rare origins
Are very hard to trace

Do you believe
God's laws are good or bad
Do you thank him for giving us those laws
Or wish he never had

Do you believe we can converse
With those who've gone before
That in our minds we hold the key
To open any door

Do you believe we travel
In the depths of deeper sleep
To a Universe beyond
In which we sometimes take a peep

When we soar along in space
And we feel that we're alone
But we somehow know we're not
We couldn't get there on our own

When our mind must be clean
For the power that we feel
Can make our thoughts at such times
On awakening, turn out real

The power does exist
And when you're in that heightened state
You can alter many things
And sometimes change the road of fate

You may think that I am rambling
But if you have been there too
You will know the things I talk about
Really are all true.

Beloved

Loving eyes behold me
Tender arms enfold me
Safe in love you guide me
I know you walk beside me

Your sweet breath upon my cheek
Your tender kiss that makes me weak
Your tender arms enfolding me
A safer place there cannot be.

Your Photo

When that face in the picture
        Smiles down at me
It uplifts my spirits
        Oh where can you be

You're locked in my heart
        And also my mind
No deeper love
        Can anyone find

I'll love you forever
        And 'though we're apart
Our love will grow fonder
        So deep in my heart

You'll always be near me
        Wherever I am
I feel you beside me
        You are where I am

Wherever you are
        I am there too
Our two hearts entwined
        We cannot undo

We both took our vows
        "'til death do us part
But I can't erase
        Your love from my heart

So I will just wait
        For the time we unite
And hope God will help us
        Through each lonely night

I'm with you in spirit
        Where e'er you may be
I hope you'll be waiting
        When God calleth me.

Through All Eternity

Do not sleep long within your grave
Just dreaming of the past
Reflecting on your memories
They were never meant to last

Do not stay long within your grave
Awaiting there for me
Do not endure the loneliness
Just waiting patiently

Just let your spirits soar on high
Your soul is free, it did not die
Your love still glows within my heart
Its flame is bright 'though we're apart

So take your place upon the wind
The friend you know so well
And gander with him freely
And thus invoke the spell

Traverse with him the time zones
Cast off your mortal shell
He's travelled all the pathways
Of mountain, stream and dell

He's wandered Earth so freely
His duties to perform
To gather all the lost sheep
And bring them safely home

The wind will take on many moods
Sometimes soft and sweet and warm
But other times, just as in life,
May ride an angry raging storm

He offers you the freedom
Of immortal liberty
To shine your light upon the Earth
So bright for all to see

To fly along gently with the breeze
Whisper sweet nothings to the trees
To sit on the boughs of mighty oaks
Shower in sweet rain as young Earth she soaks

To roam the oceans far and wide
The seas and mountains high
With seagulls flying by your side
To play and swoop and cry

Your freedom opens any door
No bonds or earthly ties
The Universe you can explore
New sights will fill your eyes

The secrets of the Universe
Once hidden from your sight
Are open now for you to view
Beyond star studded night

And when my Autumn turns to grey
And my winter time draws nigh
I know the wind will bring you back
To sweep me up on high

Then we will fly together
The way that we have planned
Our souls will mingle once again
O'er foam and sea and sand

I'll breathe your name so softly
In order to be sure
You'll hold me close and kiss me
We'll laugh and play once more

The Earth cannot contain us
As long as we are free
As hand in hand we travel
Through all eternity.

The Curtain Call

Where do I fit into this world
        And what will be my fate
Is our life's destiny unfurled
        Birth and death on a pre-set date

Do we travel along life's path
        With freedom on the way
Or is our road set from the start
        I really cannot say

But time and place must play a part
        In who we meet and why
Why some folks touch our very heart
        Whilst others pass us by

Sometimes we think we make the choice
        Of what we do and where
The people that will hear our voice
        And the love that we will share

But other times it seems to be
        We do not pick our destiny
That we are being pushed along
        A road to us that seems so long

A road that crosses other's paths
        We stop awhile and have some laughs
And then continue on our way
        To face the dawn of another day

And so from time to time we search
        For answers from beyond our birth
Far beyond our mortal skin
        The mystery of our soul within

Is this life real or just a dream
        Are we the pawns in someone's scheme
Are we the players in their game
        Which starts at birth ruled by our name

We take a break and get some rest
    And then continue on our quest
To turn back time and thus reveal
    The secrets that life does conceal

Should we question our existence
    Or take life as it comes
Should we show death our resistance
    To be picked like ripened plums

Or should we just go with the flow
    Conceding that we do not know
Our soul released to Heaven above
    To everlasting life and love

Are we just actors on a stage
    Life changing as we turn each page
No matter whether big or small
    It all ends with the curtain call.

Who Am I

I'm not always perfect
I'm not always wise
I'm someone who'll listen
But doesn't like lies

I'm someone to talk to
You know that I care
The first sign of trouble
You know I'll be there

I nursed you through childhood
I hope I'm your friend
I'll back and guide you
'til my journey's end

The person I am
Should be very clear
A loving proud parent
Who holds you most dear.

Five Years On

I sit beside your gravestone
My head is gently bowed
I speak to you in low soft tones
But I call your name out loud

The time goes by more quickly now
Than when we were first apart
My visits here much fewer now
Than at the very start

This does not mean I love you less
I miss you every day
It simply means you're in my heart
That's where you'll always stay

These flowers that I bring to you
Are symbols of our love
I know wherever I may be
You're watching from above

Each lonely night I lie in bed
And long for your caress
You're always there within my prayer
Please God your soul will bless

And so dearly beloved
This life I shall endure
Our children all still need me
And I need them for sure.

Vision or Dream

A long time ago
    I had a dream
My vision was borne
    on a single white beam

As I lay in my bed
    in a deep cosy sleep
It entered my head
    where no-one could peep

It took my soul upwards
    and whisked me away
While still on my bed
    my body did lay

I was lighter than air
    as I floated along
Over the roof tops
    and then far beyond

I should be afraid
    as I think of my plight
My companion is loving
    I know I'm alright

We stopped for a while
    to survey our surround
The buildings below
    just like spots on the ground

He took me first backwards
    where do I begin
The start of the war years
    and man's deadly sin

Or much further back
    as we soared into space
Before Earth was formed
    with no human race

The surroundings were black
    all studded with light
As the night sky on Earth
    on a lone starry night

Then over afar
    in this vast open space
An imploding star
    just went off in our face

A star which implodes
    will become so compressed
That it must reverse
    with an equal zest

The gasses and debris
    all swirling around
Attracting the items
    which share common ground

He showed me the start
    of the whole Universe
But these secrets, I fear
    I can't put into verse

We then travelled forward
    and came to my birth
He showed me the pathways
    of my time on Earth

He showed me my future
    the purpose I'm here
Should I share this with you?
    it's not very clear

So I will refrain
    from letting you see
The secrets of life
    that were given to me

But maybe some day
> I will change my mind

When people wake up
> and stop being unkind

When people start doing
> the things that they should

When killing and wars
> are washed out of their blood

And then with a bump
> I was back in my bed

The things I had seen
> would remain in my head

The vision was real
> it wasn't a dream

I'd been on a journey
> or so it would seem.

Food for Thought

God placed us all
        upon this Earth
And tended us
        right from our birth

He gave us beauty
        sight and sound
There was no need
        to till the ground

He gave us life
        and food and drink
And lots of time
        to stop and think

We did not work
        or toil or sweat
There was no cause
        our needs were met

Then men decided
        they knew best
They took God's laws
        laid them to rest

They did not want
        someone to lead them
And so God gave
        to them their freedom

A power struggle
        then began
And fights to find
        the stronger man

"You have no power
        over me
I'll be the leader
        you shall see"

To abide by rules
        they were not willing
Their hunger was
        for wars and killing

They rent and raped
        the fertile land
And turned green fields
        to dust and sand

The food that was
        in good supply
Soon disappeared
        the land was dry

And so they gathered
        slaves to toil
To sow and reap
        the barren soil

With wounds still bleeding
        famine raged
Disease and pestilence
        were soon engaged

The sick and dying
        yelled out their cry
"please God
        I do not want to die"

Too late for God
        had turned his head
He did not heed
        a word they said

For they had made
>	their choice you see
To tread a path
>	away from He

What of today
>	it's still the same
The only change
>	is the leader's name

Greed and power
>	still dominate
To keep us from
>	that golden gate

Where man-made troubles
>	rule our life
Where drugs and murder
>	cause us strife

When you recall
>	just what we've lost
Consider
>	was it worth the cost?

My Little Mate

How I miss
    my little mate
No more wagging his tail
    at the garden gate
No more big brown eyes
    and happy grin
Or welcome home
    when I come in
No more excited
    barks and yap
No more cuddles
    on my lap
No more guarding
    no more walks
No more pulling
    if we stop for talks
No more my mate
    can comfort me
No more minced meat
    for his tea
No more tripping
    around my feet
As he smells cooked chicken
    his favourite treat
No more his bark
    worse than his bite
Will alert me
    be it day or night
So I hope there is
    a place above
For a little dog
    so full of love
I hope we'll
    meet again someday
He'll wag his tail
    and we shall play.

The Power of Pure Thought

Don't ever underestimate
The power of your thought
Don't think a fleeting moment
Will just register as nought
For everything you think about
Has a real effect
Of this there is no doubt at all
So treat it with respect.

The Cost of Change (Concrete Jungle)

How have I come to hate this place
which once was green and full of grace
Where children laughed and played all day
and picked wild flowers on their way

Where fields and hedgerows, trees and streams
were places to live out their dreams
They would take their water and jam bread
and fly their kites from morn 'til bed

Or take a branch, a pin and string
and sit and fish for anything
But the happiest thing for them by far
was to bring home frogspawn in a jar

The days were long, the children healthy
they had no money, but they were wealthy
The things that nature gave were free
they did not pay to climb a tree

They did not pay for the sun and air
or sweet fresh rain that wet their hair
They did not fear the wild terrain
or the rumbling of the choo choo train

On hunting trips they'd do their best
to spot the hedgerow birds at nest
They would observe but not destroy
although some birds they would annoy

The farmers' fields were full of hay
and courting couples would in them lay
Younger children with bow and arrow
would chase the field mouse and the sparrow

Those days have gone as you can see
there is no farm or field or tree
No pond for ducks to build their nest
and hedgerows have been laid to rest

Now in this place just look around
there is no children's happy sound
No place for them to laugh and play
to recall such fun at a later day

There's sounds of traffic, screeching brakes
and juggernauts, that's all it takes
For man to make another bungle
and make instead – a concrete jungle.

With Hindsight

I never ever realised
      how much I really cared
For the person that I married
      and the life that we both shared

I never ever realised
      how much he meant to me
It's only now I've lost him
      that I can truly see

The love and laughter that we shared
      in our early days
He did not show his love in words
      but in his thoughtful ways

The many little treats he planned
      I'd often take for granted
The times we went on shopping trips
      for things I said I never wanted

Now looking back across those times
      I wish that I could say
I love you, to my sweetheart
      that would really make my day

When pressures of our life
      take over our domain
Our worries mar those days
      which we cannot live again

How selfish we can be at times
      our minds can close the door
On things that we observe
      or that we know and just ignore

A little understanding
    and help along the way
When he was feeling poorly
    could have helped him through the day

The times when he berated me
    and the hurt that I'd endure
I never ever realised
    that he was hurting more

He often used to ball and shout
    his anger, he'd let reign
His way of dealing with his life
    when he was feeling pain

But underneath the charade
    of the way that he would scold
Was a feeling, caring, gentle man
    with a heart of gold

Don't let the pressures of this life
    dictate the way for you
Don't let your love fade with the strain
    but keep it strong and true

If we could only stop a while
    and take a deeper breath
We'd understand the love we shared
    could never end with death.

Don't

Don't waste your life just wishing
      for the things you'd like to do
Don't sit around just hoping
      that your dreams will all come true

Don't waste your life pretending
      that you are something that you're not
Or be jealous of your friends
      because you want what they have got

Don't wait around for fortune
      to come knocking on your door
You can sit around forever
      and then end up on the floor

Be positive in your thinking
      do not shirk in what you do
The achievements that you gain in life
      are really up to you

For life is for the living
      not for the feint at heart
If you want the things you're wishing for
      you had better make a start.

When Can We

When can we let our children roam
    To smell sea air and watch the foam
To play in sand and build their castle
    Without the fuss and all the hassle

To play in fields and bales of hay
    While the farmer looks the other way
Or let their thoughts drift off in dream
    As they sit in silence by the stream

To lay upon the cool green grass
    Gazing at clouds as they quickly pass
To hear the crickets no one sees
    Or smell the blossom on the trees

To chase the butterflies and bees
    Or take a tumble on their knees
Or pick the flowers growing wild
    As I did when a little child

Alas no more their freedom reigns
    As paedophiles pursue their aims
And danger lies at every door
    Not caring whether rich or poor

When can we let our children roam?
    Instead of saying "stay at home
Where we can keep you in our sight"
    And "No you can't go out at night".

A Walk in the Park

A walk in the park
With my love by my side
He's holding my hand
I feel full of pride

My heart feels uplifted
As we stroll along
With sweet smell of blossom
And sound of birdsong

We chase through the woods
I hide near a tree
It ends with a kiss
He captures me

We stroll further on
Take a boat on the lake
We capture the moment
With the photos we take

We now take a rest
And sit by the stream
Enraptured in talk
Discussing our dream

There's no better feeling
When two hearts entwine
He knows I am his
I know he is mine

These things are just a memory
They happened long ago
I'm sitting in my armchair
And basking in the glow

My love has left my side now
After fifty happy years
I remember all the good times
It helps hold back the tears.

What is Love?

Love is
    the basis of everything
Love is not a word
    but purity of heart

In a pure heart love abounds
    love works by deeds but not in sounds
Love moulds our thoughts and shapes our living
    love grows in strength by the art of giving

Love is the truth of little children
    love is the honesty we build on
Love is peace of body and mind
    love excels in being kind

Love is the power of good over evil
    the love of God wards off the devil
Love has no place for cheating and lying
    with each bad deed our soul is dying

Love is the food that feeds the soul
    love is the blessing that makes us whole
Love is the way to life everlasting
    keep love in your heart and give without asking.

Life Continues On

I may ask you
> What do you believe?

You may answer
> Nothing. If there's a God why does He watch me grieve?

I may ask you
> Why do you feel sad?

You may answer
> Because I miss my Dad

I may ask you
> Why do you feel blue?

You may answer
> With my loss, you would too

I may ask you
> Where did you get your seed?

You may answer
> From both my parents, I concede

I may ask you
> If what you say is true, do not they both live on in you?

You may answer
> That's very plain to see. The mirror shows I'm off their family tree.

I may ask you
> Would you rather see them suffer, if you had a choice?

You may answer

Oh! I see you've lost your voice.

Wholeness

One heart, one mind
One body, one soul
These are the things
That make us whole

Without the heart
We cannot live
Without the mind
We cannot give

Without the body
We cannot function
Without the soul
There's no compunction.

Children

What can we give a little child
    when we're entrusted with their life
How can we teach them how to live
    a life of love that's free from strife

We can hold them in our bosom
    through the darkness of the night
And keep them safe and warm
    until the early morning light

We can nurture them and feed them
    we can show them that we care
We can let them know we love them
    and for them we're always there

We can help them with their reading
    how to enjoy their days at school
We can do this without pleading
    or being taken for a fool

We can teach the need for cleanliness
    and the art of being smart
It helps to build their confidence
    and can uplift the heart

When sometimes we admonish
    we should explain the reasons why
We're here to help them understand
    not to make them cry

We can help them to be youthful
    and to sing a happy song
We can teach them to be truthful
    when their troubles come along

We can teach the art of talking
    conversation can be fun
We can listen to their troubles
    making time when day is done

We can teach them to tread wisely
    on a straight and narrow path
And laugh their way through hard times
    whilst they are silencing their wrath

We can help them to stand firmly
    and learn not to be afraid
When they are confident and happy
    they'll no longer need our aid.

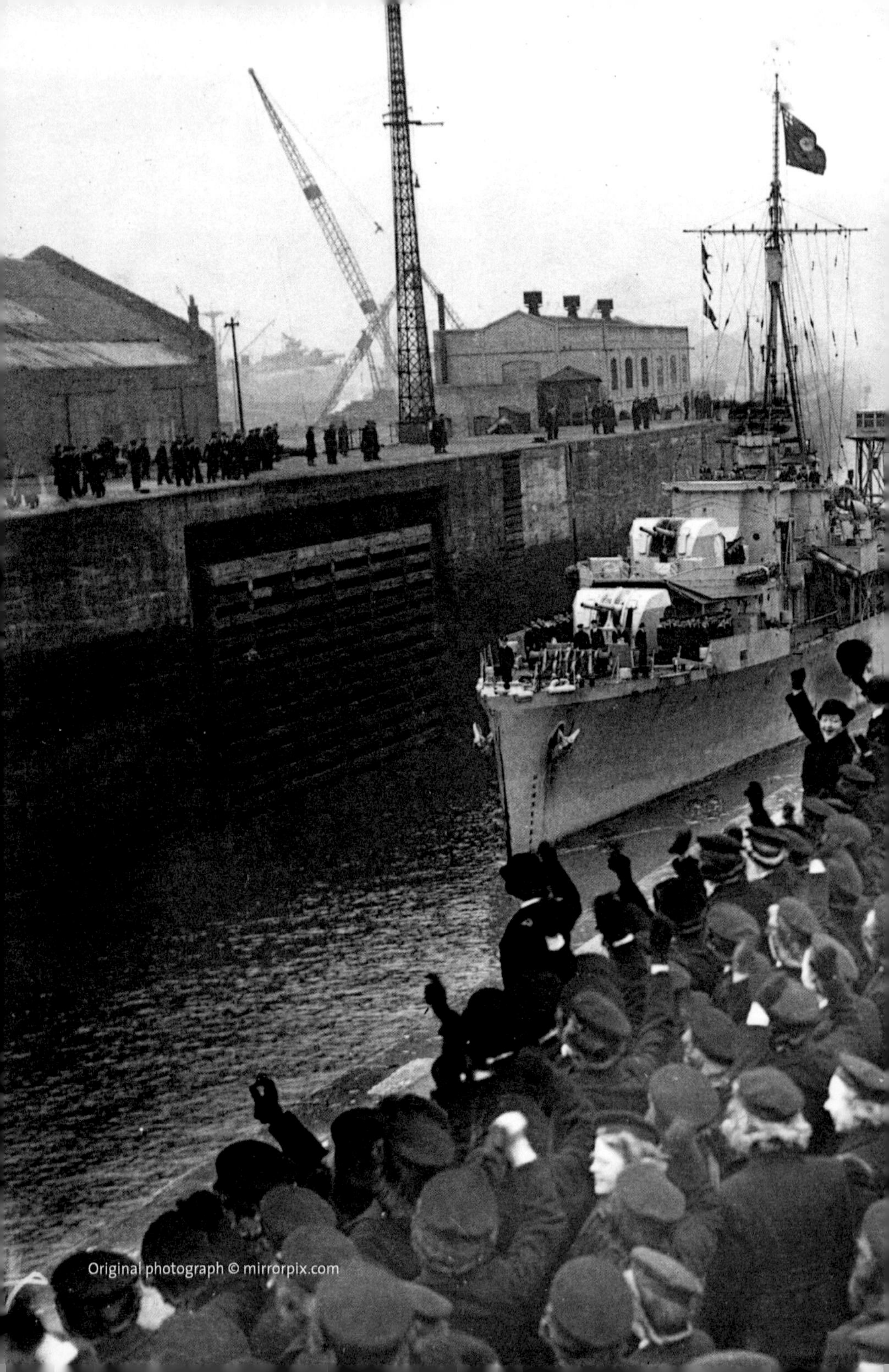

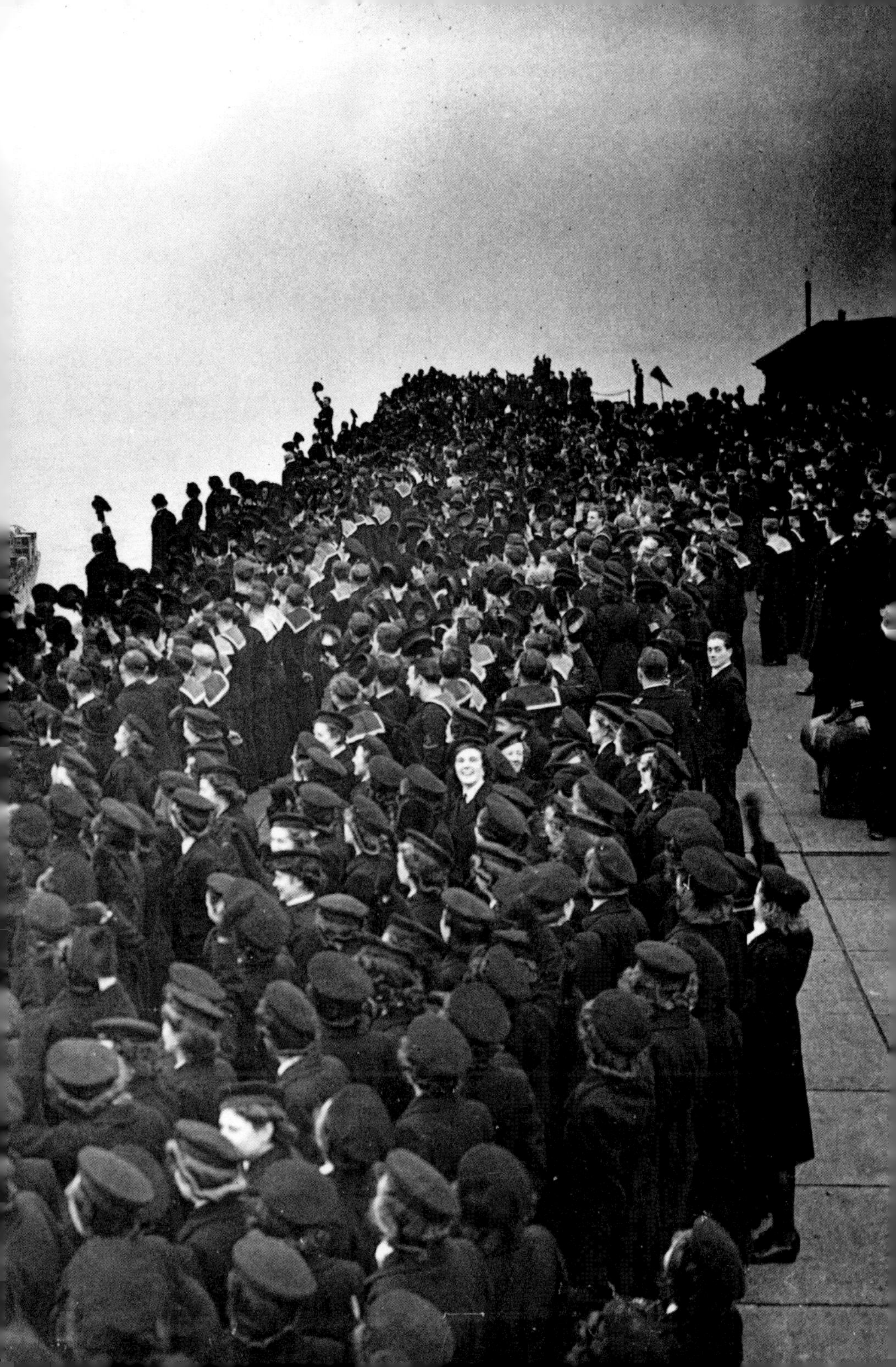

Friends

In this land of living
        everybody needs a friend
A shoulder they can cry on
        or perhaps an ear to lend

To rejoice with them when happy
        a rock when they are sad
A friend who stands beside them
        when the good times turn to bad

A friend who lifts their spirits
        when they are feeling low
If you can help them have a laugh
        you will watch their troubles go

You can help them make decisions
        their confidence to build
You can let them know they're not alone
        and help them be strong willed

And when it comes to marriage
        your best friend should be your spouse
If you show each other that you care
        you will build, on rock, your house

So keep these thoughts within your heart
        when you are looking for a mate
Be true and honest from the start
        and do not trust to fate

For trust and understanding
        are the secrets of success
And health and fame and fortune
        will add to your happiness

Remember to be loyal
        their confidence keep true
If they can trust your honesty
        then they'll be there for you.

Deeds

Each good deed done
That remains untold
Will reap you rewards
Deed – times tenfold
But if you consider
Kindness doesn't pay
You will find what you have
Will be taken away.

Life

We set out on the road of life
on the day that we are born
All equal on our birth date
mother's egg and father's spawn

Then begins our journey
in the lottery of life
Our background forms our future
born into fame and fortune or poverty and strife

We cannot choose our parents
we do not have a voice
It's up to them to set our road
we do not have a choice

They may be kind and caring
and help us on our way
Or leave us in the hands of fate
just living out their day

But there will come a point in time
for us to walk alone
To make our own decisions
on the things that we will own

If we are wise we may have learnt
the lessons that it takes
From others that have trod their path
and not make the same mistakes

We cannot plan with certainty
the road that we will tread
We may have to change direction
just to earn our daily bread

We may have to cope with illness
or traumas in our life
We may lose someone we care for
or face the surgeon's knife

But no matter what the future holds
or what our dreams may be
Our life is our most precious gift
and life was given free.

Into the depth

I climbed into my bed one night
    the night was cold and dark and still
I tried to ease my frenzied sleep
    and exercise my will

I tossed and turned in restless sleep
    there was a sneezing in my ear
I felt that I was wide awake
    but it was not very clear

Then I was falling into darkness
    I wondered what to do
And as my body gathered speed
    a river bank – came into view

Then falling, falling, falling
    terrified I'd hit the ground
Falling deeper, deeper – now in water
    with the fear that I'll be drowned

Clinging, clinging onto grassy bank
    I cannot get a grip
As grass keeps slipping from my grasp
    I feel like a sinking ship

The bottom's looming closer
    I do not want to die
"Help oh help" I try to shout
    to someone passing by

But no-one's there to hear my voice
    or help me in my plight
It seems I do not have a choice
    I may pass away – tonight

To cross beyond the mortal bounds
    of Earth and sea and sky
To hear the sound of Angels song
    as flapping wings pass by

To cross the sea of Blackness
    above the starlit sky
And leave behind the sense of fear
    as new sights greet my eye

I want to raise my voice and shout
    to scream up to the sky
But my voice, I find, is in my head
    I can't even raise a sigh

Then all at once I give a gasp
    and then begin to cry
Someone has shocked me into life
    the light now hurts my eye

It was not death that beckoned me
    to take me from this Earth
I realised – with bated breath
    I was witnessing – my Birth.

Think Twice

Think twice before you act
upon a niggling little whim
Don't do something you can't retract
when you're upset by her or him

Remember that your actions
will impact on your relation
The answer to your problems
might be the art of conversation

Don't think the world abounds
around just you and all your feeling
If you don't consider others
then you can't begin the healing

At times it seems we all endure
that feeling of neglect
But in our hearts we know
we don't convey what we expect

If you don't face a problem
with your life or with your mate
Then the molehill grows much bigger
and your love might turn to hate

If you truly seek the answers
to a fulfilled and happy life
You'll stand steadfast by each other
through the good times and the strife

Loyalty and understanding
makes love stronger you will see
The foundations you can build on
are trust and honesty.

Cosmic Twin

My spirit soared on high one night
    it raised above the cloud
It travelled quicker than the wind
    which soared and wailed quite loud

I watched the buildings disappear
    as if by magic they were gone
My vision now was very clear
    as my spirit travelled on

Far, far into the Universe
    I have been this way before
The difference that I witness now
    is the opening of the door

Instead of light there's blackness
    pitch black as darkest night
I cannot see in front of me
    it seems I've lost my sight

But although I cannot see
    what lies before me as I fall
I feel that I am travelling down
    a long and narrow hall

I say that I am falling
    as that seems the way to me
But my spirit is not solid
    so it surely cannot be

And then I see a glimmer
    a spot of light comes into view
How far this time have I travelled
    what will I learn anew

I focus on the spot of light
    and wonder what I'll do
It now seems very clear to me
    it was a black hole, I passed through

I'm feeling quite excited
    my mind is racing free
Then all at once – I reel in shock
    there is another one – of me

The surroundings are familiar
    although something is amiss
I try to make my presence known
    but I don't succeed in this

I stand and face my other self
    I have a scar above my eye
A mirror image faces me
    I don't understand the reason why

I raise my hand and touch her arm
    she shivers as I do
She seems to sense my presence
    but does not know what to do

How can I communicate?
    how can I get through
Has she travelled down the path
    that I have travelled too

Or did she take another path
    that I chose to ignore
Are all our pathways open
    for each one – to explore

I can't get her attention
    my time here is running low
I <u>will</u> try to come back again
    but just now, I have to go

Do we travel many paths?
    all living side by side
Are there many more dimensions
    in which each of us reside

If I should travel out again
    pass through <u>another</u> door
Will I find another one of me
    slightly different from before

My body now is calling me
    I've been away too long
My silver chord, now too far stretched
    is pulling me back strong

I travelled backwards urgently
    no time to mess around
And suddenly I'm back in bed
    without another sound

I'm back to face reality
    my feet back on the ground
From this day on my cosmic twin
    will always be around.

Growing Up

Through each generation
you'll oft hear folks say
'Twas better than this
in my younger day

The things they remember
are what touched their heart
Those memories within them
with which they won't part

We remember the good times
forgetting the bad
And all close our eyes
to what we never had

We relish the changes
that improve our life
And point out the bad things
that now cause us strife

We tell all the young folk
you don't know you're born
Overlooking their problems
their hearts might be torn

In each generation
a problem is real
And no-one can know
what each of them feel

Our lives run in cycles
or so I have found
With fashions repeating
themselves all around

The seven year cycles
that start from our birth
With bodily changes
in stature and girth

The emotions we feel
when these changes take place
And all of our feelings
are shown on our face

We all have our ways
of handling our lot
We don't trust our peers
for they may have forgot

The feelings inside
with each changing day
Our secret anxiety
the price we must pay

But each generation
all go through the pain
Of teenage illusions
that they're very plain

The teenagers cry
I'm too fat or too thin
I don't like my hair
or my pimply skin

I don't like my eyes
or the shape of my nose
I don't like my legs
or the style of my clothes

We fancy someone
they don't know what they've missed
It's all in our mind
as we've never been kissed

Then someone shows interest
we don't know we're born
We laugh and we sing
from bright early morn

We think we're in love
all excited inside
It shows on our face
though we all try to hide

We go through a phase
when people all tease
Our blushes show through
as they ignore our pleas

And then we grow up
as if overnight
We've got through our teens
and now we're alright

Then we sit and reflect
as time passes by
Our childhood has gone
in the blink of an eye.

War Child

When we think of times within the past
    our childhood in the war years
We remember many bad things
    things that reduce us all to tears

The bombing and the poverty
    the lack of teachers and education
The lack of both our parents
    in their aim to help the nation

With our fathers in the forces
    and mothers working to help war aid
The children had no guidance
    and we often were afraid

The blackout was a problem
    no house ever showed a light
If the air-raid siren sounded
    we would all run home in fright

The house was dark and empty
    often without a fire or food
There was no-one there to meet us
    or help dispel our mood

The winters were so very cold
    with coal in short supply
And if we got our clothes wet
    we had no way to get them dry

Our cups were odd and mainly chipped
    and some had lost their handles
With no money when the light went out
    we relied upon night-lights and candles

If we made a pot of tea
        we had to let it stew
As tea-leaves were in short supply two
        they were used more times than

For sugar we had saccharin
        a tiny little pill
Which we also used in cocoa
        no wonder we were ill

Instead of margarine
        we used dripping on our bread
With a little pinch of salt
        or perhaps jam toast instead

Our washing day was Monday
        with washing tub and boiler
With dolly pegs and dolly blue
        and starch to do the collar

We did not have a lot of clothes
        perhaps a change or two
You could not know how hard it was
        unless you'd lived it too

We did not really understand
        the fact that we were poor
Even when the rent man came
        and we hid behind the door

We put cardboard in our shoes
        to help our feet keep dry
But it didn't really work
        and our socks were stained with dye

Our kitchen floor was concrete
    and we didn't have a mat
The other rooms had wooden floors
    with lino upon that

The condensation on the windows
    and the water on the pane
The excitement in the morning
    when Jack Frost had been again

We often had no hankies
    though we'd have a running nose
Newspapers torn up for the loo
    but that was just how it goes

We often had no breakfast
    but we had to go to school
If we turned up late each morning
    we were threatened with the rule

We picked our way through rubble
    with bomb-sites all around
With shrapnel, bombs and bullets
    strewn with goods upon the ground

Our clothes were never warm enough
    our hands and legs turned blue
With chilblains in the winter
    there was nothing we could do

So don't be discontented
    with the things that you have got
Compare it with our childhood
    and you'll see you have a lot

But although the times were hard
      it wasn't always bad
We didn't have the time to care
      about the things we never had

The people were more friendly
      and the children all would play
It didn't matter who they were
      they were a child at end of day

I am writing down this record
      to help you understand
The price we paid for victory
      of this green and pleasant land

And when the war was over
      it didn't end the score
As the rationing continued
      for a further ten years more.

Single Parent

How sad I am that I should see
the troubled times surrounding me
When single parents seem to be
the norm in my locality

With married couples hard to find
and others part and do not mind
Instead of sorting out their rows
they throw away their holy vows

With little children's feelings
tossed aside without a care
The parents and the home
that with them both, they cannot share

The confusion that they feel inside
when Mum or Dad has gone
Two parents sitting side by side
for them, there's only one

Special days shared, to them denied
when birthdays come and go
What happened to their family
they may not ever know

How often do we hear the cry
"my Dad will sort you out"
But they are only empty words
for Dad's nowhere about

They may be put in foster care
or even in a home
They may have no-one to turn to
though too young – they stand alone.

Family Tree

It's amazing what you find
    when you trace back your family tree
You can't get very far
    without it costing you a fee

But if you're of the mind
    to find out where you are from
A computer might just help you
    when you start your own dot.com

The first thing you must do
    is start with your own birth
But be warned before you start
    there may be skeletons to unearth

When you have your own certificate
    you should be feeling glad
It will give the details of your birth
    and name your mum and dad

It will include their address
    and give your mother's maiden name
And your father's occupation
    is put into the frame

Information on your siblings
    can be important too
They may have been born elsewhere
    and give a clue to you

The next stage is your parents
    the year and place that they were wed
If you haven't got the facts right
    you may trace someone else instead

The marriage lines will tell you
    some more things you need to know
Their father's name and occupation
    if you don't already know

It will also give you details
    of their age as like as not
And both their place of residence
    before they tied the knot

Repeat this code of practice
    with each parent and their line
Be patient with your research
    and things will turn out fine

And then there are their siblings
    if you find that you can't trace
Check the details on their papers
    and things might slot into place

You may be very lucky
    when following your search
You may find that they've been static
    not spread out to any girth

This can be a bonus
    and your pulse may start to race
As you find that generations
    are confined to just one place

But some names are quite common
    you should check your facts with care
You can overlook the obvious
    and think that they're not there

As you gather information
    and you learn the family trade
Some stories that you may have heard
    may turn out to be self-made

Whatever you find out
    don't expect a legacy
For the most of things in this life
    are rarely given free

Don't go looking for a fortune
    if you share the same surname
As someone rich and famous
    you may end up looking lame

You'll often feel excited
    and sometimes lose the plot
When you think someone's related
    then you find out that they are not

But if you are related
    and you truly find a link
They may be pleased to see you
    and invite you for a drink

You may find family members
    who have been researching too
If you give them information
    then they will share with you

You might get tired of searching
    when you come to a dead end
You might just leave it at that point
    or consult a learned friend

When you've checked the Record office
    births, marriages, deaths and wills
And you've checked through old church records
    you might just need their skills.

The Headless Chicken

Around and round
    And round and round
        The headless chicken ran

Around and round
    And round and round
        Trying to escape the man

Oh tell me headless chicken
    Why do you run so fast
        Your life is nearly over
            You cannot make it last

Around and round
    And round and round
        The headless chicken went

Around and round
    And round and round
        Its life was almost spent

Why do I run so fast you say
    Away from that awful man
        If I escape his clutches
            I won't end up in the pan.

Young Lives Lost

Spitfire pilots – just young boys
spitfire planes their brand new toys
How many hours in the air?
just a few, fine, sign right there

Now you are here, check out your plane
how many markers will you gain
How many strikes will be your claim
not even one. Ah! that's a shame

Now get some sleep we fly at dawn
prompt and sharp no time to yawn
We're flying in the second wave
chin up boys, look like you're brave

I'm your leader follow me
stay in line now, one, two, three
Up and at 'em come on boys
it's time to play with your new toys

Leading, diving, blinding sun
fingers slipping off the gun
Dog fights! Flirting with the Hun
is that another battle won?

Count the young ones flying back
seem ok- but some took flack
How many this time have been killed
their space at table must be filled

On standby now so grab some sleep
you've lost your mate – no time to weep
Follow me – you know the drill
feeling sick – just take a pill

Search lights stab and sirens wail
dodge him son, he's on your tail
Twisting, turning hit the ground
another crew that can't be found

How many of ours did we lose
we need more rookies to fill their shoes
How many more boys will meet their death
or come home burnt but still draw breath.

No Pockets in a Shroud

We all look for the Brightest star
    when the one we love has gone
We hold their souls, they can't go far
    they are all we focus on

Our minds cannot accept our loss
    nor friends dispel our fears
Those moments when we say we're fine
    but can't hold back the tears

We're in a trance, an unreal state
    we wonder what will be our fate
Then fear and anger, guilt and blame
    all take their turn in the grieving game

We pray each night to God above
    to save the soul of the one we love
To raise them as a child of light
    and let their glow be strong and bright

In our hearts they hold a special place
    we wish that we could see their face
Our heads bring memories to the fore
    we hold them in our arms once more

Sometimes we weep, sometimes we smile
    we'll soldier on, just for a while
We vow to live a better life
    to help someone in their daily strife

To understand each other's needs
    and aim to only do good deeds
To set our goals and not be vain
    for bad deeds only lead to pain

There is no place for us to hide
    so we take each day within our stride
We teach our children right from wrong
    and gain pleasure from their happy song

Material gains all have their place
    work hard, gain them with God's grace
But do not neglect your hungry soul
    combined, head and heart will make you whole

Life is precious, live it well
    a full life leaves a tale to tell
Your family loves you, make them proud
And remember-
    there are no pockets in a shroud.

The Wind

The wind tapped on my window
very gently one fine day
It seemed that he was calling me
to tempt me out to play

I stepped outside to welcome him
but thought, he cannot speak
So how can I converse with him
then, he gently kissed my cheek

This was the beginning
of our friendship – cast in stone
Whenever I am feeling low
I know I need not be alone

Each time that he entreats me
and we raise towards the sky
He blows away my troubles
and lifts my spirits high

Oh wind come down and gather me
I am longing for a ride
Can I come along with you
or will I, this time, be denied

I understand that sometimes
your anger, you must let reign
If I come along at such a time
I might not get home again

To my delight he hears my plea
and gives a mighty roar
I quickly don my hat and coat
and tumble through the door

He bends the bough of a mighty tree
I climb up and on his back
The birds disperse in disarray
then follow in his track

The wind now steps it up a pace
we are racing through the trees
At the speed that we are travelling
the branches scrape my knees

It's getting more exciting
as we rise above the cloud
I'm clinging on for dear life
but I'm feeling very proud

Oh tell me wind my dear friend
what lies in store for me
Will you tell me tales about the old times
before I came to be

Or will we travel silently
as you incite my mind
Leaving my imagination free
to see what treasures I can find

This time, we push the clouds
it seems they're fighting back
They are denser and more heavy now
their centres turning black

There is a rumbling of thunder
and lightning passing by
But in the arms of my dear friend
I am cosy, warm and dry

I am feeling quite elated
my confidence now glows
I love to travel with the wind
as around the world he goes

We travel on at speed now
we are racing with the storm
It's getting very dark though
so he decides to bring me home

We cut across the moonlit sky
over mountains topped with snow
As we travel over roughened sea
I watch the waters ebb and flow

Then as my home comes into view
he sets me on the ground
He will travel all alone now
on a new journey, he is bound

But he will come my way again
as he hears me beg for more
Adventures, balanced on his wings
over hill and dale and moor

So until that time I'll be content
to spend my time with you
And say "Thank you" to my friend the wind
my thoughts still fly with you.

Unity

Our hearts lead us
    to paths of good
Our heads when not in unison
    often lead astray

Our hearts feed souls
    the way they should
Our heads confuse the issues
    and cause conflict on the way

Let's not ignore our heart's desire
    or follow paths of greed
Let us not hurt others
    in pursuance of our needs

Let us not love in word alone
    but in our acts of deed
Let us not turn our head away
    pretending not to see a child in need

Let us not fear ridicule
    because we show compassion
Let us not follow like a fool
    the current trend or fashion

Do not be cowardly in your quest
    for justice and for good
Do not sit silently or say
    I never understood

Let us all pursue our lives
    helping others on the way
Let us all remember to Thank God
    in prayer – for each new day.

Poetry Society

A local poetry society
    announced an open day
Please come along and join us
    you do not have to pay

I had jotted down some verses
    but was not sure what to do
When a friend of mine encouraged me
    saying "I will come with you"

I took along some poems
    perhaps a moment would arise
For me to get some feedback
    and then to my surprise

I was greeted quite warm heartedly
    and asked to play a part
I enquired how I should react
    she said "just recite it from the heart"

It's my turn to recite now
    I'm feeling like a fool
My host introduced me to the crowd
    as the "Pam Ayres of Liverpool"

My neighbour was responsible
    it was she who coined the phrase
But I was apprehensive
    as I hadn't earned the praise

I wish I had Pam's talent
    I wish I had her wit
I'm on my feet committed now
    so here goes. This is it

I try to judge the company
    which poem should I choose?
Will they enjoy my effort?
    or will it all end – with boos?

Too late to change my mind now
    I try to sound off-beat
The theme I choose is humour
    it all goes down a treat

My confidence is boosted now
    the crowd all shout for more
I rattle off a few more lines
    they are rolling on the floor

The host's face was turning redder
    she tried to subdue the crowd
"It's time to take a break now"
    she said to me out loud

"Our society is quite sombre
    we're not used to having fun"
As she thrust a cup of tea at me
    closely followed by a bun

It seemed I had caused chaos
    folks were laughing all around
Instead of being serious
    with feet firmly on the ground

When the interval was over
    it was time for me to go
Time to gain composure
    and as a smile begins to show

My host announces loudly
    "you're a genius with the pen
We've all enjoyed your company
    but please – do not come again"

Angels

Angel of Mercy
Angel of Light
Came down from Heaven
And gave me a fright

Angel of Mercy
Called out my name
Angel of Light
Put me in the frame

I saw my past
But only the flaws
These are the things
That make up our scores

Things from beginning
To end of our life
Thoughts that we harboured
When suffering strife

Feelings of anger
Feelings of fear
Why this should be
It's not very clear

Things that were minor
Not worth second thought
Things we thought hidden
To front mind are brought

All things are known
And although you may frown
You'll know I am right
If you should start to drown

Your life flashes by
But just seconds have passed
You know you may die
But you hope life will last

Angel of Mercy
New hope you have brought
Angel of Light
Flashed up a new thought

Here is your chance
Time to review
You can turn your life round
It's all up to you

Don't harbour hatred
Nor jealousy feed
Don't harm other people
For fortune or greed

Don't hold a grudge
That eats up your soul
Learn how to forgive
And make yourself whole.

Old Friend

It was in the Springtime dear wind
    when first you came to me
The birds were singing sweetly
    there was blossom on the tree

You tapped upon my window
    you sensed I'd lost my way
You beckoned me to come outside
    and join you in your play

I knew I need not fear you
    as you rushed up to the tree
We were both feeling lonely
    now you had found a friend in me

My heart was beating faster
    my pulse began to race
A gentle breeze was blowing
    as you kissed me on the face

I was longing to go with you
    as you danced around the cloud
I thought it was impossible
    and would not be allowed

But then you came and gathered me
    you raised me on your arm
I knew that I could trust you
    that you meant me no harm

I shall not forget the journey
    you took me on that day
You helped me overcome my fears
    my troubles passed away

You stripped away the darkness
    that overshadowed my domain
You showered me with kindness
    and helped me see again

You helped me face the loneliness
    and chased the blues away
Why you chose to befriend me
    I really cannot say

But I am grateful for your company
    and everything you do
I realise with heavy heart
    that you are lonely too

We have enhanced the friendship
    that was wrought on that first day
I know that you can't linger long
    but must be on your way

And I must go on living here
    until I loose this mortal tie
When my ethereal spirit floats on up
    to join you in the sky.

When I was a Child

When I was a child
    the meadows were green
With hosts of wild flowers
    you may not have seen

The butterfly hoards
    of all colours and kinds
All fluttering by
    and pleasing our minds

The lovely blue sky
    with white fluffy clouds
The soft grass below
    with no maddening crowds

As we lay in the grass
    with the clouds high above
We let our minds drift
    with our hearts full of love

When young love developed
    through touch and by sight
And hearts were awakened
    on dance floors at night

Romance played a part
    and courting was fun
With bright moonlit nights
    or warm sultry sun

A love formed by nature
    oh! What a delight
On bright sunny days
    or on star studded night

These things will all pass
        as man breaks his new ground
You can then search forever
        but, once lost, can't be found

How glad that I am
        I was blessed and could see
The beautiful things
        God created for me

I pity the future
        generations we sow
The sights and the feelings
        that they'll never know

So take heed you people
        who think you know best
Developing problems
        in your eager quest

To make our lives better
        as seen in your sight
You will be among us
        and share in our plight.

The Wretched Child

A child lies crying in his bed
    his whimpers cause a stir
There's rats or mice beneath his bed
    but no-one else is there

He's terrified he needs the loo
    but can't get out of bed
Although he tries to hold it
    he wets himself instead

He's feeling cold and frightened now
    wondering how to hide the mess
When his mother smells the urine
    she's surely bound to guess

If he gets through until morning
    it might have dried a bit
He'll say "I've done it in my sleep"
    and try to use his wit

He knows this will not save him
    she'll make him strip the bed
Saying "take it down and wash it"
    as she clouts him on the head

There isn't much for him to do
    as he only has one sheet
So he puts it in the bathtub
    and stamps it with his feet

As he struggles to the wringer
    which is very hard to wind
There is a trail of water
    that is following behind

Then as he gets the bucket
        and mops up the wet floor
His mother comes to check on him
        and knocks him with the door

He has to go to school now
        the start of a new day
But sometimes he plays truant
        and simply stays away

He's frightened now to stay indoors
        he much prefers outside
Although it's dark and cold out there
        no vermin there reside

He sits upon the kerbside
        and plays the waiting game
The cold strikes through his backside
        and haemorrhoids start to pain

His mother ventures home at last
        God knows where she has been
She's dressed to kill as usual
        she thinks she is the Queen

On finding him out in the street
        her anger soon shows through
He knows what's coming is no treat
        she'll beat him black and blue

She takes the whip she's hidden
        then takes a breath or two
"If you can't respect my wishes
        I'll knock it into you"

She takes the whip and starts to lash
      his young and tender skin
With threats to put him in a home
      if he does not stay in

He tries to heed her wishes
      he is not really bad
He wondered what life would be like
      if he had of had a dad

But he is just a little boy
      and all he craves is love
He tries to mend a broken toy
      and looks for help above.

Fishing with Dad

A little boy was crying
as he climbed into his bed
I want to see my daddy
but they tell me he is dead

Last Summer we went fishing
and we had a lovely time
He taught me how to bait a hook
and how to cast a line

We sat beside a camp fire
as he told me tales of old
Of the days he spent with Grandad
of camping in the cold

He taught me how to light the fire
gut and cook the fish we'd caught
He taught me many more things
he was very good at sport

But then the war had started
and I could not understand
Why my Dad had gone away from me
and not done the things we'd planned

I recall my mother crying
when his call up papers came
His words were "Don't you worry darling
I will soon be home again"

"This war will soon be over
there are enough of us to fight
We will put a stop to Hitler
when we show him England's might"

But as the time kept passing by
with no end of war in sight
We had to carry on with life
as did many others in our plight

We braved the bombs and rations
and learnt to scrimp and save
To make my father proud of me
I promised I'd be brave

I'd do my very best at school
and help Mum with the chores
And then Dad would come home again
when they'd put an end to wars

We would all be back to normal
to do those things we'd planned
Dad would take me fishing
and I would hold his hand

Before I went to school one day
there was a knock upon the door
My mother went to open it
then fainted on the floor

I wondered what had made her scream
when the telegram arrived
It gave the news that Dad was dead
whilst some others had survived

I will always have my memories
but when you're only ten
It's hard to know my Dad and I
will never fish again.

Over the Rainbow

Let's all fly away to a faraway land
where troubles are turned into small grains of sand
Where wealth is the fortunes of sun, sea and air
and everyone smiles and they haven't a care

Where everyone's happy and people don't fight
and no-one's afraid of the darkness of night
Where children are safe and they can run free
please take hold of my hand and come there with me

This place does exist, it isn't a dream
just over the rainbow and down by the stream
Where the sun shines its brightest at break of the day
with birdsong and laughter of children at play

Where people all work for the things that they need
there's no room for squabbles and no place for greed
Where everyone helps and there's no need to ask
and all take their turn of the menial task

Come over the rainbow to that faraway land
where everyone's equal and no-one is grand
God's Garden of Eden, placed here upon Earth
and all Human Kind, knows just what they're worth.

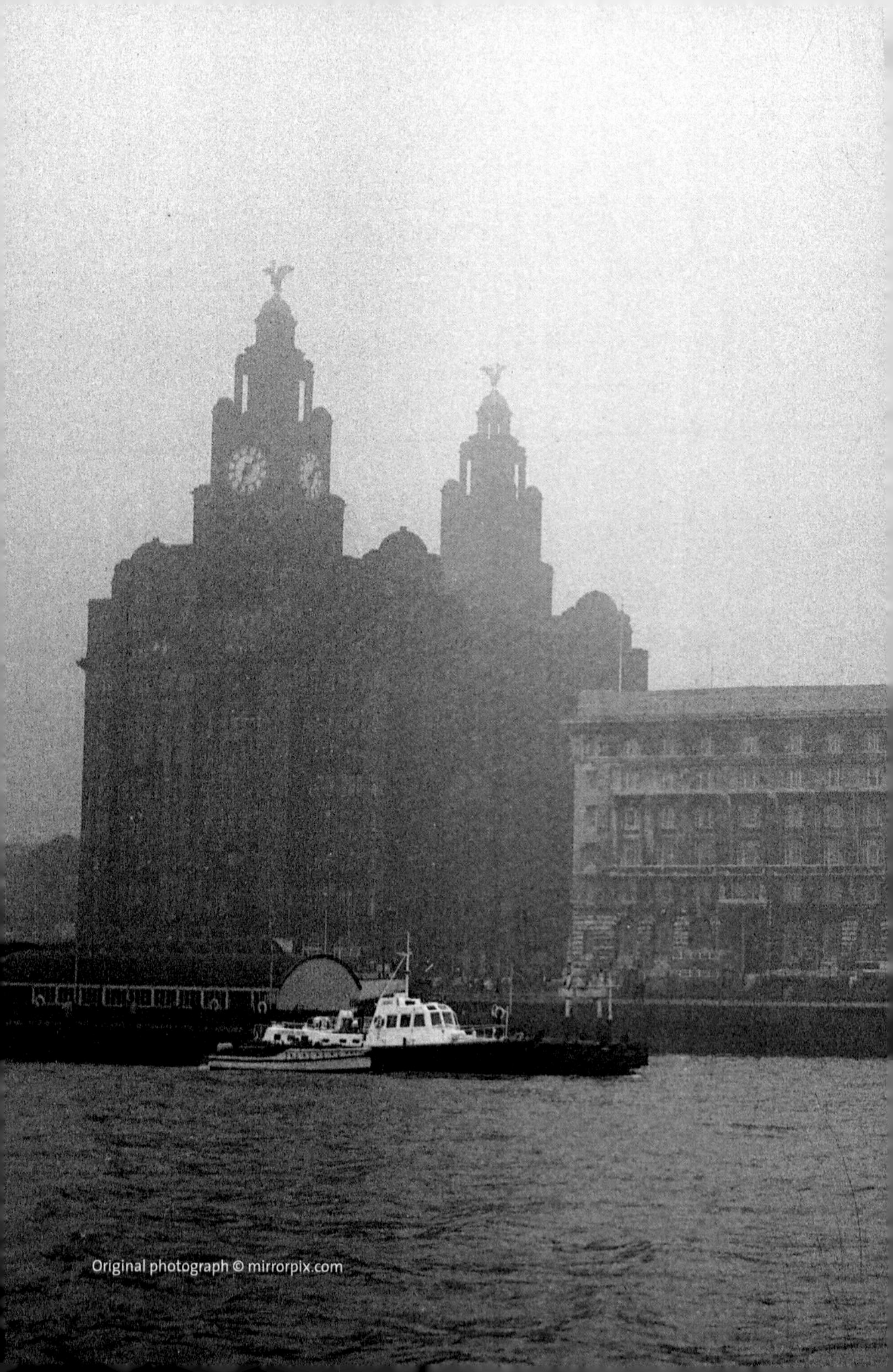

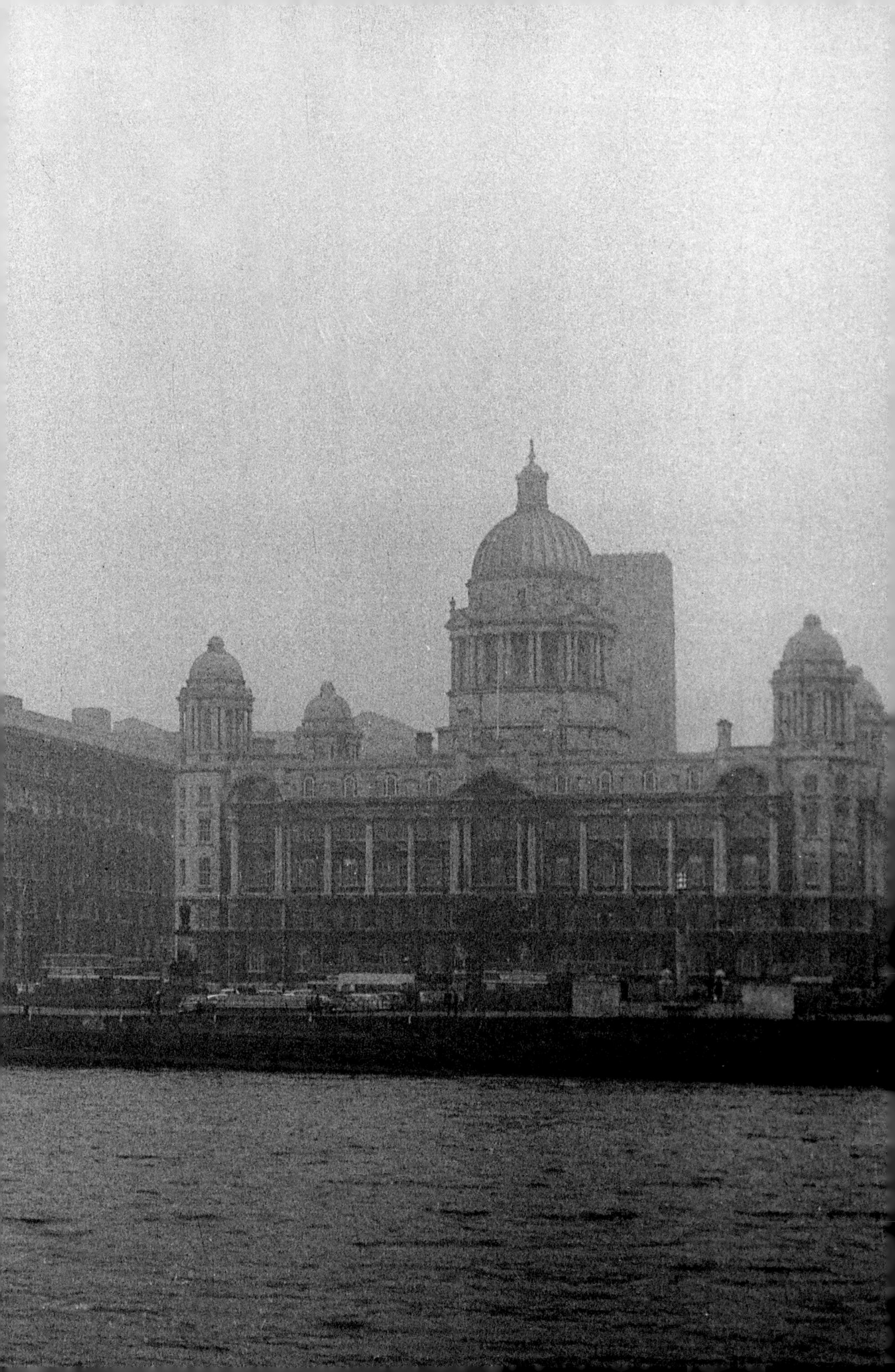

Children's Minds

The land of little people
exists in children's minds
Goblins, elves and fairies
of every shape and kind

Sometimes they are happy
and with them love to play
But sometimes they are frightened
in bed at end of day

They may want to keep the light on
as they lay there in their bed
You cannot make them understand
their fears are in their head

So have a little understanding
if your child should show such fears
Stay with them and just comfort them
don't let them go to sleep in tears

Remember your own childhood
and the things that made you glad
Nothing makes a child feel safer
than a loving Mum and Dad

Tell them a happy story
when they go up to their room
Make sure their favourite teddy
is there to dispel their gloom

If your child is feeling happy
when they go to bed at night
They will sleep so soft and soundly
that they won't wake up in fright.

A Whim

I'd love to write a book one day
but I don't know where to start
Should it be a tale of love
concerning matters of the heart

Or should I choose adventure
each chapter wrought with fear
Or venture into unknown realms
of gambling dens and beer

A thriller could be lots of fun
twists and turns upon each page
A murder plot uncovered
by an old detective sage

A children's book of learning
of having lots of fun
But when I put my mind to it
I find it has been done

There's history with lots of things
that one could write about
But facts must all be accurate
of this, there is no doubt

So this is just a whim of mine
one day it might come true
I have no knowledge to write crime
but then again – do you?

One day I might surprise myself
just write what's in my head
But at this very moment
it is time to go to bed.

A Wise Man Watcheth

There was a very wise man
who resided on a cloud
His hair was white and flowing
and he wore a bright blue shroud

As he perused the Human Race
the people never saw his face
They would not see him passing by
mid- fluffy clouds and deep blue sky

For they were too aloof and proud
as they mingled with the flowing crowd
With stiffened necks and heads held high
to see their observer passing by

They hurried on to their abode
not seeing the cloud on which he rode
From whence he watched the Human Race
pursuing their goals at a deadly pace

He watched their antics and shook his head
entering their minds as they slept in bed
He tried to influence their brain
to save this race from going insane

They did not heed what they had seen
instead they said "It's just a dream"
And so they continued to pursue
the things that they ought not to do

As they forged along their roads to fame
politicians and Generals owned no blame
Riches and power would be their lot
as they schemed and planned their deadly plot

Wars and hunger, tears and strife
all became part of their daily life
The orphaned children's tear stained face
became the norm in this war strewn place

To influence the public
they used their hosts of spin
And then confront the people
with their false and sickly grin

They probe the whys and the wherefores
of the people that they meet
And poll public reaction
from the people on the street

From this they get a feeling
of how far that they can go
If they can fool the people
they can watch their ratings grow

When they get a bad reaction
and they know they've gone too far
They create a new distraction
for the young, a new pop star

For others, there is football
or any other sport
They'll even close their eyes to crime
as long as they're not caught

And so their greed for power
notoriety and fame
Destroys them by the hour
with no remorse or shame

The wise man watched from up on high
he shook his head and gave a sigh
He could not save the Human Race
for they had perished in disgrace

He could but save a very few
the good and honest, me and you
The pure of heart, the meek and mild,
the orphan and the unborn child.

The Girl on the Swing

There was a little girl
who was playing on her swing
When at the bottom of the garden
she spied a fairy ring

She was looking very hard
to see what she could see
When all at once a fairy
landed on her knee

A pretty little fairy
in a lovely bluebell dress
She cried out to the little girl
"my wings are in a mess"

"If you would like to help me
I'll tell you what to do
And if you fix my wings for me
I will do something for you"

The little girl was happy
to help her little friend
And she collected gossamer
the fairy wings to mend

The little fairy kissed her
and whispered in her ear
"You may come and visit us
and we won't need to fear"

So early in the morning
when the adults were asleep
The fairy called the little girl
and told her she must creep

She crept into the garden
down to the fairy ring
And when she saw the fairies
they all began to sing

They made her Queen of Fairies
and gave her a blue dress
To take back to her bedroom
and out into a press

They granted her three wishes
she said "I'll just have two
If instead of having number three
I can still be friends with you"

Then everyone was happy
and everyone was glad
But she had to keep their secret
only tell her Mum and Dad.

My Friend the Wind

What ails you now my dear friend?
do not huff and puff at me
You are like a jealous lover
when other friends I see

You know that I adore you
our friendship's true and strong
But when you have your job to do
I cannot string along

We have to go our separate ways
throughout stages of our life
But the bond we forged so long ago
will remain all of my life

When I was young I loved to feel
your breath upon my face
That gentle unexpected touch
just like a sweet and warm embrace

In Spring you helped to wash my face
with the sweet soft gentle rain
And then you blew the rain away
and the sun shone bright again

Summer was a time for fun
the sun would rule the day
A time for you to have a rest
or sometimes come and play

Late Autumn you had work to do
helping trees to shed their leaves
I sometimes travelled with you
on journeys such as these

In Winter you turned very cold
your anger you'd let reign
Mourning friends from long ago
you would never see again

Spring came along and anger passed
then as the season played a part
You travelled back to visit me
and once more touched my heart

So please do not be angry
when other friends I see
They cannot dent the love that's there
twixt my true friend and me.

A Grandmother's Sorrow

The hurt I feel and sad at heart
to see this family torn apart
The little children's small sad face
as they wake up in some strange place

The hugs and kisses that I knew
are gone from me along with you
I cannot tell you how I'll miss
your smiling face and spitty kiss

No matter what the future holds
from sad grey days or streets of gold
From kindergarten into teens
and dressing up in your best jeans

The days will pass so quickly by
you'll sometimes laugh and sometimes cry
There's something I want you to know
a Nanny's love will never go

Although we may be far apart
you will remain within my heart
And no matter where you go or do
I will always have a place for you.

The Hanger On

I am jealous of your beauty
I am jealous of your fame
I'll pretend that you're my true friend
and I will use you for my gain

When you show up at a party
your popularity abounds
When I try to make an impact
I'm just pushed to the background

You're the centre of attention
among the happy throng
I cannot get a word in
so I tag myself along

I will listen to your secrets
and put them in my store
And when I'm feeling angry
I'll have tales to tell galore

If I really want to hurt you
I will add a little more
I'll make your life a misery
And make sure that you don't score

But when the party's over
and the people start to shun
I know I've lost your friendship
and I'm missing out on fun.

Who am I

I was born into this family
with a loving Mum and Dad
My childhood was not perfect
sometimes good, and sometimes bad

Where did I get my looks from?
Where did it all begin?
The colour of my eyes or hair
the colour of my skin

The shaping of my future
or the paths that I would tread
The things that I should nurture
or how I'd earn my daily bread

Who made the decisions
that would influence my life?
A life that could be carefree
or of never ending strife

Where do I fit into this world?
What truths along the way unfurled?
Which path to take- the left or right
my thoughts race on throughout the night

Shall I go on chasing shadows
and trace back my family tree?
No. For the answer to Who am I?
Is simply – I am me.

Do You Ever

Do you ever get the feeling
that you have done some things before
It may just be coincidence
or it may be something more

Do you ever get the feeling
there's someone you long to meet
Then the person you are thinking of
comes walking down the street

Do you ever think of someone
when you are sitting all alone
And the person you are thinking of
simply rings you on the phone

Do you ever visit somewhere
that you have never been before
But know what will be waiting
when you open up the door

Do you ever stop and wonder
why this happens just to you
You think you've done it all before
it may very well be true

You may <u>think</u> that you're the only one
that these things happen to
If you talk to other people
then you'll find they feel it too

So what can be the reason
for these strange feelings in our lives
Should we just forget them
or for answers, should we strive

Could it be our lives
are all recorded from the start
and then the tape rolled backwards
when we are born, to play our part.

Open up your Mind

The mysteries of life
are not too hard to find
Just concentrate a while
and open up your mind

The answers to the questions
that you are searching for
Are buried deep within you
along with many more

For when you find one answer
then you open up the door
And your seeking grows much deeper
there are many questions more

The Universe is infinite
and as you travel in
You'll find that you are travelling
to where it and we begin

You may find that you feel frightened
when you sense you are alone
No-one can travel with you
you can't reach them on the phone

But if you can relax awhile
and just go with the flow
You'll find you'll get the answers
to the things you wish to know

The answers to the Universe
not just the Human Race
The knowledge that you seek
will stare you in the face.

A Sound Direction

Respect and moral fibre
are in short supply today
With many doing what they like
and going where they may

Parents fight each other
and children follow suit
They should just nip it in the bud
before it takes strong root

The stress and strains of living
in the rat race of today
Leave children lost and floundering
they're told to go away and play

This may mean isolation
as they sit up in their room
With no-one there to talk to
their future takes on gloom

We all need a sound direction
a place to head in life
With love and understanding
not hopelessness and strife

A goal to set our sights on
a dream we can achieve
A parent to rely on
who does, in us, believe

So if you never had the chance in life
to make your dreams come true
Don't take it out on children
remember – they belong to you.

Air Raid

The sirens screech
        another raid
No time to get
        the table laid

No time to eat
        for we must run
Or take a pounding
        from the hun

There are shelters dotted
        here and there
Some folks pass by
        and do not care

Some folks stay
        inside their homes
Trying to ignore
        the bombers' drones

Blackout curtain
        pitch as night
No house ever
        dared show light

The drone of bombers
        in the sky
We pray that they are
        just passing by

The little boy laying on
        cold tiled floor
Trying to dig a hole
        making both hands sore

He was trying to
        escape the din
Wondering what
        had been his sin

Some older people
> curse and swear
Seeking shelter
> anywhere

Railway stations
> underground
Many people
> there compound

Barrage balloons
> fill up the sky
To catch the planes
> as they pass by

Never having
> much success
But helping people
> ease their stress

Dust and debris
> on the street
Who moved the ground
> beneath my feet

What made my stomach
> twist and turn
The siren's screech
> when will they learn?

Search lights stabbing
> out their light
In search of planes
> at dead of night

Wardens shouting
> don't come near
Until the siren sounds
> All-clear

Buildings burn
      and bodies bleach
Water hydrants
      out of reach

ARP in force
      all night
Aiding people
      in their flight

An injured person
      on the ground
Calls out a name
      they can't be found

A child is calling
      for his Mum
But she lies dead
      and cannot come

A policeman stands
      with tear-stained eye
Still trying to prove
      big men don't cry

As he moves a shoe
      which contains a foot
That churns his stomach
      and his gut

Some people did not
      leave their house
But hid inside
      like a timid mouse

They prayed and prayed
      that they'd be spared
But alas sometimes
      nobody heard

I ask you
    what is the point of war
What is this power
    we're fighting for

What kind of person
    do we breed
Who must fulfill
    their urge for greed

This urge for power
    over man
Can we not contrive
    another plan

Or be thankful for
    the things we've got
It seems to me
    that we cannot.

Our Die is Cast

From conception to birth
our die is cast
We know not our future
nor our past

Some of us are planned
with loving parents blessed
They nurture us with love
into a cosy nest

Some of us
of married couples born
Not planned, by accident
they sowed our spawn

With mixed emotions
they await our birth
Our environment helps
to shape our place on Earth

Some of us
by single mothers planned
Unsuspecting fathers
of a one night stand

Perhaps to fulfill
their needs of motherhood
Perhaps for financial gain
not for our good

But once we take
that first sweet breath
We must travel along life's path
until our death

We must live out our life
for all it's worth
We must not waste a minute
of our time on Earth

But no matter how or why
our seed was bred
The time will come
for us to make our bed

A time for us to choose
the way we live
A time to thank our parents
or perhaps forgive.

The Cost of War

When I was just a little child
shy and quiet, meek and mild
My father went away from me
to fight the war with the army

He was with the expeditionary force
(the war will start in due course)
He did not know how long he'd spend
fighting this war from start to end

I did not know where he had gone
for as a child, life carries on
I started school, my first day there
a wooden desk and wooden chair

My teacher wore a flowered smock
a smile upon her face
I gave a sigh, my knees did knock
as she showed me to my place

I was fairly quiet
my confidence was low
When would I see my Dad again
I really didn't know

I cannot quite remember
my early days at school
Was I fairly clever
or did I sit there like a fool

Then one day a surprise
as Dad came knocking at the door
But it was just a little respite
he had to return once more to war

The days went on
turned into weeks
The death knoll tolls
the air just reeks

Bombs were dropping day and night
when sirens rang out we'd run in fright
Our shelter was not very good
a hut of tin, a door of wood

Outside our house a landmine hit
a crater where a lake could fit
We were in bed but still awake
and as it hit, our house did shake

There was a knock upon the door
we had to go, with many more
The warden came to usher us
along with others, to a bus

We went to a church not far away
but only stayed there for a day
We were among the lucky ones
some folks were killed with smoke and bombs

The church was hit the following night
and some of those that shared our plight
Never saw the light of day
as most of them were blown away

The drone of German planes
above us in the sky
Making our hearts pound
and all our mouths feel dry

The talk of paratroopers
dropping in the night
And the warden's heavy footsteps
giving us a fright

With fathers in the forces
and mothers out at work
And little children fending
for themselves without a shirk

The sight of all the debris
on our way to school
And then the empty chairs
which then became the rule

I've been deprived of all my childhood
my parents and much more
My father was a stranger
when he did return from war.

Honour the Fallen

We honour the fallen
we honour the brave
To give us our freedom
their young lives they gave

Amid all the bedlam
amid all the din
Alone and afraid
they would not give in

Through nerve gas and vomit
they answered the call
They rose up and at 'em
though many did fall

Their families at home
knew not of their plight
They remembered their loved ones
in prayer every night

The trenches were sodden
troops cold, wet and damp
But they carried on fighting
ignoring their cramp

They carried on fighting
by night and by day
The loss of their life
the price they would pay

And so we remember
the good and the brave
And honour the fallen
with each poppy and grave

But we also recall
the ones who came back
With broken minds and bodies
no courage did they lack

And to end this short verse
I would just like to say
"Thank you" to all those
who gave me my today.

The Lonely Soul

A lonely heart
A lonely soul
Who wanders far
To find its goal

Another dawn
Another day
Another soul
That's lost its way

It gathers height
It gathers speed
Follows the light
To fill its need

The light will lead it
On its way
As down below
Its family pray

Then all at once
It's gathered in
Welcomed by love
And free from sin

A soul that's gathered
In the night
Can now become
A child of light.

Just the Mist

The house is dark and empty
its walls are old and grey
The furniture which once stood grand
now slowly rots away

Large tapestries adorn the wall
now faded, damp and torn
Ancestral pictures once looked proud
but now they seem forlorn

With doors and windows shattered
the rain and frost creep in
Now half the roof is missing
it really is a sin

In each room the cobwebs beckon
increasing more each dawn
Wildlife have their freedom
I have even seen a fawn

The once delightful garden
now overgrown – bereft
It never has been tended
since the last of family left

How sad this feeling of despair
for times that have long passed
The happy times that once were shared
too bad they could not last

For times were good in times gone by
when laughter rang out loud
And children's voices filled the air
among the happy crowd

When precious family gatherings
were rituals not to miss
And adolescent cousins took a chance
to steal a kiss

When lengthy meals were over
the family would then split
The ladies to the parlour
to gossip, sew and knit

The gentlemen would stay a while
to drink and have a smoke
They would then argue politics
or tell a smutty joke

The children would be rounded up
and taken for a walk
A stroll around the garden
while nannies had a talk

The older children trusted to do
just what they may
As long as they were home in time
for bed at end of day

The family had resided here
nigh on two hundred years
But family life had ended
when they had to leave in tears

For it soon became a scandal
the presumed "killing of a friend"
A body floating in the lake
brought the party to an end

The family never breathed a word
of how they'd lost the lot
And no-one ever proved a case
of a blackmailed murder plot

With no money in the coffers
the family moved abroad
The house was left to rot away
"No squatters" said the board

They hoped they could return one day
when the scandal had died down
But every time they showed their face
they were greeted with a frown

And I am just a "ghost of time"
who struggles to exist
when sometimes people see me
they say
        "It's just the mist".

The Queen

One day my young grand child
was starting to brood
So I asked her what problem
was causing her mood

She sat down beside me
and looked in my eye
Then asked me quite loudly
"Does the Queen ever cry?"

I was taken aback
by the sudden concern
About the family so regal
which she now wished to learn

I answered her question
she knows I won't lie
"We all show our sorrow
when one of us die

So to say that the Queen never cried
would be quite absurd
As everyone does
despite what you've heard

No public display
is the way they are trained
No matter how happy
no matter how pained

But when she's alone
her emotions run free
The Queen is still human
just like you and me".

Warm and Cosy

One night I was laying cosy
warm and cosy in my bed
The night was calm and quiet
as I lay down my weary head

Then all at once a wind blew up
the tree outside began to sway and creak
Some branches were blown from the tree
for they were old and worn and weak

The wind began to play with them
and tossed them in the air
But some went thudding to the ground
the wind just did not care

His mood was dark and angry
as tree and bough he bent
You could not reason with him
until all his puff was spent

I could just sit and watch him
dance with the tree in playful fight
Or allow him to disturb my peace
make this a restless night

But I was warm and cosy
warm and cosy in my bed
So I simply closed my eyes once more
and went to sleep instead

He could howl outside my window
and make endless things take flight
But he could not tempt me from my bed
on that warm and cosy night.

Moving On

A memory
    I cannot share
The reason why
    I was not there
I'm not a part of
    Your yester-year
Those early days
    When you knew fear
I am part of
    Your here and now
And I will help
    To show you how
To clear the cobwebs
    Of the past
And let your mind
    Be free at last.

Soul Mate

I said a prayer the other day
you know I often do
To thank God for those precious days
he let me share with you

Those happy sultry summer days
when two hearts beat as one
And all the world was ours to share
our time had just begun

Those early, carefree, mystic days
we longed for time to meet
With pounding hearts and bated breath
walking on clouds, the air beneath our feet

Though all the streets were crowded
my eyes saw only you
And as we shared a sweet embrace
I knew that yours were blinkered too

You'd steal an unexpected kiss
and send a thrill right down my spine
Whispering love words in my ear
to let me know that you were mine

The love and laughter that we shared
is felt by just a few
I bless the day you came my way
and I fell in love with you

Spring and Summer were our heydays
until the Autumn came around
Soon your Winter time had darkened
and the sun could not be found

We waited for the final call
we knew it can't be long
But through the pain and sorrow
we vowed that we'd be strong

And through our tears
with vision blurred
We'd show the world
how much we cared

How strong still now
our love shines through
As part of me
goes forth with you

My future is uncertain now
without you by my side
But as the years go drifting by
I sense you there to guide.

Tomorrow

If we could know tomorrow
and the changes it may bring
It can maybe bring us sorrow
or make us want to sing

If we could see today
what tomorrow has in store
We might change the state of play
on the plans we'd made before

If we could have rehearsals
enact tomorrow out today
Correcting our mistakes
for which life really makes us pay

If we could shape our future
and avoid the stumbling blocks
We could help each other find a way
to avoid life's many knocks

If we could just rehearse
even one day at a time
We may change the Universe
there may even be less crime

If we could see our future
the effects our actions bring
It may make us sit and ponder
before doing anything

We sometimes get an inkling
intuition, fate or dream
But that doesn't really help us
as we're not sure what they mean

But life does not allow us
when tragedies occur
To turn the clock back on our lives
and say we're sorry we weren't there

If we could show the ones we love
how much we really care
Not keep taking them for granted
because we know they're always there

But we cannot see tomorrow
or the traumas it may bring
Though we can all change our actions
to be prepared for anything

We can decide to follow
the feelings of our heart
Then we will carry no regrets
when the time does come to part.

Original photograph © English Heritage (Aerofilms Collection)

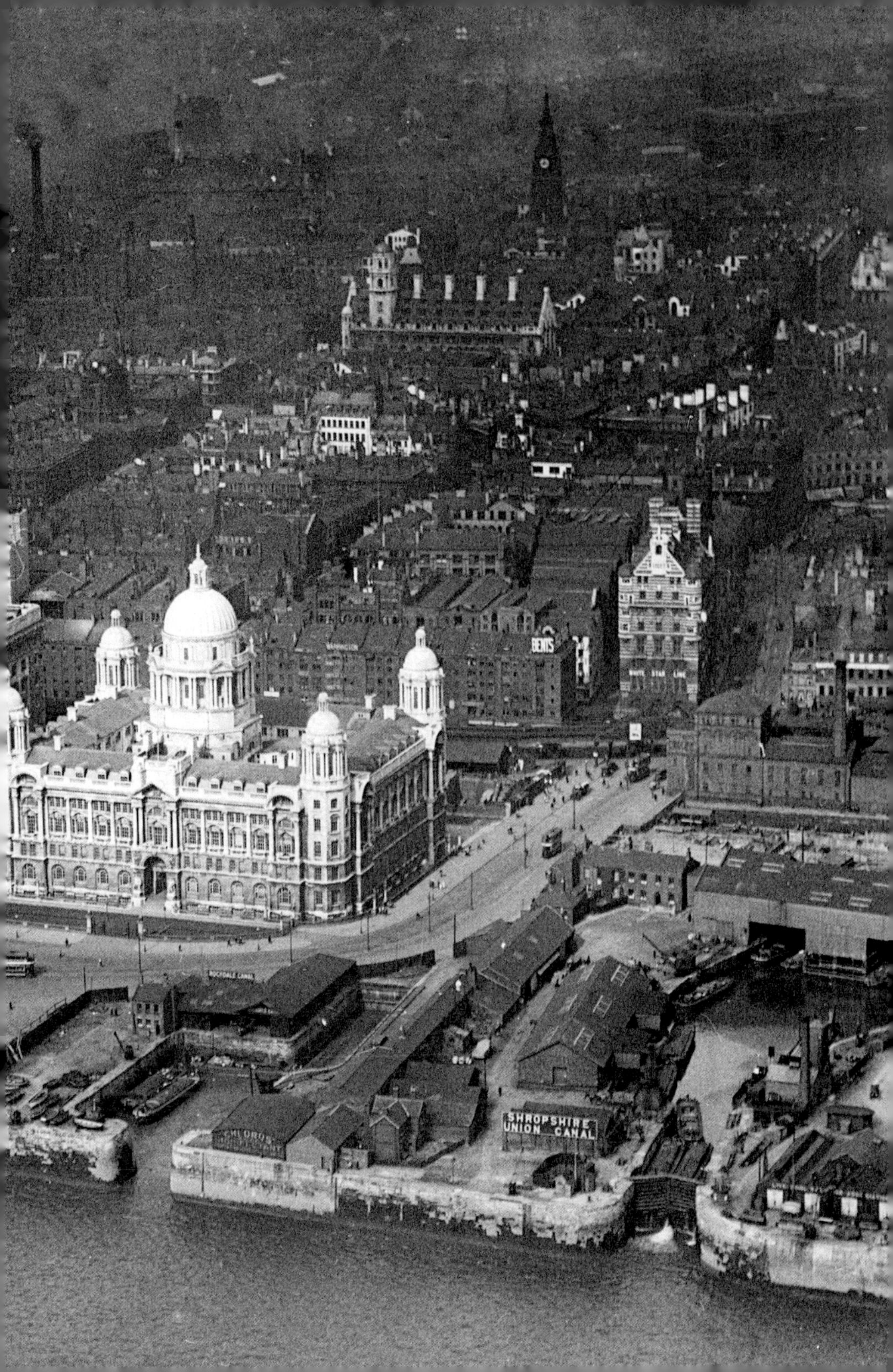

A Poem for Rita

She is my skin and blister
She is my only sister

When we were young we used to play
Those games that children do
Top and whip and hopscotch
Swinging around the lamp post too

Hide and seek and knick-knock
String tied to the neighbour's door
If we saw the "Bobby" coming
We would run away for sure

Kick the can and Sallio
Who has got the ball
Skipping was a favourite
Or two balls against the wall

Playing in the garden
With tennis bat and ball
Crickets hopping around our feet
We didn't mind at all

Find a four-leaf clover
Or make a daisy-chain
"Do you like butter?" buttercups
We'd play now and again

Easter came with Spring time
New pumps and gingham dress
Auntie Eileen made them
Her talents to express

The red hot sun in Summer
Would really melt the tar
Sometimes we would fall over
But it rarely left a scar

Autumn brought the wind of change
When trees would all change colour
Collecting leaves down Orrel Lane
To see what treasures we'd discover

Lots of snow in Winter time
When hats and coats we'd don
Snowball games and snowmen
Would all add to the fun

Just a trip down memory lane
To days we cannot live again
To carefree days when we were free
To the games we played, both you and me.

A Soldier's Child

The little child looked up at Mum
And asked her why she cried
Her heart was clearly broken
That could not be denied

The mother hugged her little one
And tried to hide her pain
She had to say that Dad was dead
But how could she explain

For Daddy was a soldier
He was used to taking knocks
He had even faced the prospect
That he may come home – in a box

And so he'd left a message
For the child he loved so dear
To let them know how much he cared
That he would try to stay – quite near

Look up at the stars tonight
See how bright they shine
Look up at the stars tonight
And tell me that you're fine

Hold your Mummy's hand
As you stand beside my grave
Hold your Mummy's hand
And help her to be brave

I know you're feeling lonely
I know you're feeling sad
I know you have no daddy
And you wish that you still had

But you have still got a daddy
Even though we're far apart
You have still got a daddy
I live forever in your heart

If ever you should need me
You'll feel me standing by
I'll come closer to your ear
And give a little sigh

So look up at the stars tonight
See how bright they are
I'm with you in the stars tonight
I'm never very far.

An Imprint

We all leave an imprint
On our journey through life
No matter how brief
No matter how slight

We all leave an imprint
Like a footprint in the sand
No matter how lowly
No matter how grand

It starts with a cry
As we take our first breath
And ends with a sigh
On the day of our death

The time in between
Records all our life's span
The good and the bad
Of each child, maid or man

Yes the time in between
Is where we make our mark
It registers clear
During both light and dark

Some marks may be shallow
Some marks may be deep
But they all have a place
Even in the realms of deep sleep

Each movement we make
Each feeling we feel
Each thought that we think
All record as real

So bear this in mind
With each step you take
On your journey through life
With each decision you make

If you bear this in mind
When watched from above
Your imprint on Earth
Will be laden with love.

Quick Quote

Don't close your eyes and
pretend you can't see
When people are hurting and
of help you can be.

Remembrance Day (Eleven Eleven)

It seems like only yesterday
I wrote a poem for you
Another soul that's gone away
whose dreams will not come true

You hoped to make a difference
to stop life being shed
You would help to ease the suffering
but you lost your life instead

So many wasted lives
so much time apart
So many broken ties
and now a broken heart

You gave your life for freedom
but the fighting still goes on
How many more will perish
as you come home one by one

And side by side we bless the souls
of All who've gone before
Most of all we pray to God
to put an end to war

We stand here and salute you
as in your grave you lay
Honoured as a hero
on this Remembrance day

So until this world is safer
and All nations make war cease
Until All men strive together
May you
       Rest in Peace.

Soul Mates

A stranger sat across the room
and looked in my direction
A stranger sat across the room
their expression showed affection

I smiled back across the crowded room
to let them know I understood
There was a mutual attraction
it seemed we both shared kindred blood

Though not a word was spoken
two souls became entwined
No word of mouth is needed
in the language of the mind

When soul mates meet each other
two hearts begin to beat as one
There is a lifting of the spirit
as though life has just begun

A single glance alerts the soul
then knowing eyes connect
It soon becomes apparent
each other's thoughts, they can detect

But if they are bespoken
they may simply walk away
Treasuring the moment as a token
with the hope they'll meet again – someday

But other times if they're both free
they tread the road that's meant to be
And so it was – with you and me
and now we share a family tree.

The Hankey Clan

How many years will this book span?
Property of the Hankey clan

How many times will it be read?
To ponder on things that I have said

How many people may play their part?
And add some words from their own heart.

The Garden

Look out in the garden
What can you see?
Masses of blossom
On the sweet apple tree

Look in the garden
What do you spy?
The buddleia tree
With bright butterfly

Look in the garden
The pond is alive
With fishes and frogspawn
How well they all thrive

Stand still in the garden
What can be heard?
The rustle of trees
And the sweet song of bird

Go walk in the garden
Feel the warm sun
Play out in the garden
And have lots of fun.

Teenagers

Although we always love them
we dislike their lazy ways
But were we any different
in our younger days?

Our parents did our laundry
our meals were always there
They would ask us to be tidier
but did we really care?

Maybe care is not the word
that I should really use
For at that time within our lives
we did not share their views

Loud music from the bedroom
clothes strewn across the floor
A growl from under bed clothes
as we call them through the door

Spending hours in the bathroom
before that special date
If you want to spend a penny
they will say "You'll have to wait"

Loud banter from the siblings
sometimes a banging door
"What is going on up there?"
we bellow with a roar

But when we feel frustrated
that they won't get out of bed
We hear them coming back at us
those words our parents said

We now repeat those phrases
which we did once ignore
We've turned into our parents
as now, our offspring, we implore

So instead of getting angry
with your children as we do
Just enjoy the good days
when they spend some time with you

One day their turn will surely come
then you may hear them say
"I've turned into my parent
somewhere along the way".

Old Oak Tree

I saw a bird
    on an old oak tree
He kept on calling
    "Look at me"

I raised my eyes
    to where he sat
Then all at once
    I saw a cat

The cat was
    crawling stealthily
Along the branch
    of the old oak tree

The bird kept
    singing merrily
He felt as safe
    as he could be

His heart was full
    of love you see
As he built his nest
    in the old oak tree

The cat had dinner
    on his mind
A tastier dish
    he could not find

He crept along
    the branch once more
With bated breath
    and outstretched claw

The bird was calling
       to his mate
But would cat's dinner
       be his fate

I then let out
       a mighty roar
To save him from
       that deadly claw

The frightened cat
       turned tail and ran
The bird called
       "Catch me if you can"

The bird did not
       fall to his prey
He flapped his wings
       and flew away

The cat now firmly
       on the ground
Crept past the form
       of a sleeping hound.

Child of Light

I am the soul of a still born child
whose spirit did not die
I hover over an empty shell
and watch my parents cry

I cannot go back to that shell
my existence to regain
So I will just wait patiently
in case my chance comes round again

Sometimes when things like this occur
there seems to be no reason why
When parents say "It is not fair
why did our baby die?"

But there will be a reason
why we could not survive
A flaw within our make up
perhaps too early we arrive

Ignorance and negligence
can sometimes play a part
Or as in many cases
they could not start our heart

But do not be down hearted
as our mortal shell you grieve
Our soul will rest in Heaven
until once more, you can conceive

I wish to reassure you
as you lay awake each night
My soul was taken upwards
to become a child of light

My light will shine upon you
you may sense that I am near
I feel your love surrounding me
I know how much you care.

The General

The General was a quiet man
A Royal Inniskilling
He did not smoke
He did not drink
And never went with women
And when they came to honour him
And most of them were willin'
To canonise and make him a saint
But he'd spoilt it with all the killin'

The Headless Man

There was a man in Egypt
Who was born without a head
He never closed his eyes at night
And never went to bed

They hung him in the wardrobe
But never locked the door
They didn't mind him hanging there
Because he didn't snore

They washed his feet in quick lime
For they began to smell
Because he could not see
To fetch the water from the well

By morning they had vanished
His feet, that is, for sure
When they saw his predicament
They simply locked the door

So if you go to Egypt
To find the headless man
You'll find him in the wardrobe
A standing on his hands.

This Little Book

This little book without a pen
Was sent to me in 2010
Without a pen I could not write
And so the page stayed blank all night

When morning came I made a pact
To fill these pages using tact
To write about a thing or two
And hope the subjects interest you

Before I start I'll find a pen
And hope the words will flow again
I'll sit right down and make a start
And hope that I can touch your heart

If you can laugh or even smile
Forget your troubles for a while
If I can help you carry on
Then I can say my work is done

A little praise, a little prayer
Can help you cope when I'm not there
But until that time has come around
You know just where I can be found

A book doth have a life you see
And can last through eternity
And through its pages there may be
A tiny little bit of me.

My Little Book

I found this book
Inside my drawer
Then thought that I
Should write some more

Or you may think
My life was blank
My brain was just
An old think tank

So I will try to
Sound quite wise
And hope my words
Open up your eyes

Some words to make
You stop and think
Set down your thoughts
With pen and ink

You've lived a life
And there must be
Some thoughts
To span eternity

For words when
Written on a page
Have their own life
And know no age

Historians like to
Find a thread
Of how we earned
Our daily bread

If you jot down
Some thoughts each night
It might help them
To get things right

There are many records
Of the wars
But not of people
And their chores

Of people's hopes
And many fears
Of happiness
Or maybe tears.

Quick Quote

Let Angels of Heaven
remain by your side
And Wisdom and Truth
with you shall reside

The Star

I stood on the edge of the forest
On guard 'til the following morn
I was in the British army
Alert, but a little forlorn

The sky was a beautiful midnight
The moon had that silvery hue
And all of the squadron were sleeping
Each armoured and each of its crew

Yes all of the lads they were sleeping
A squadron of armour and all
Lay hidden in the forest
I only had to call

And if I should call with a warning
Or fire my Lee-Enfield at all
They'd respond with an urgent sensation
Like a madman may dance at the ball

The engines would whine as they started
Then break in a heavier roar
As searchlights stabbed out in the darkness
And orders were shouted galore

But all of the squadron lay sleeping
And all was silent and still
As I shouldered my Lee-Enfield
And wandered on up the hill

I stopped and gazed up to the stars
Of clusters clear and bright
Some shone it seemed like they were blue
While others shone quite white

It was then that I witnessed it moving
And I couldn't believe my own eyes
One star had dropped down from the heavens
And was dancing around in the skies

Yes it floated on down from the heavens
Like a leaf as it falls from a tree
It floated on down from the heavens
And took a great interest in me

It seemed aware of my presence
Though I could not determine how
And hovered just over yon treetops
In my mind, I can still see it now

It was bright as a fire enfolding
And round as a star looks to view
But was eerily, silently moving
It was silent, and nothing I knew

The hair on my neck stood up proudly
The sweat round my beret was new
But my legs seemed more than willing
To hurry on back to my crew

Then another squaddy came running
He had witnessed the very same sight
Let us hightail it back to our unit
We have both seen enough for one night

The light o'er the treetops shone brighter
Then shot straight back up in the sky
In size it became quite diminished
Then soon it was lost to our eye

We wondered if we should report it
We both knew how crazy we'd sound
Perhaps someone had a new weapon
To spy upon troops on the ground

We had to report to the sergeant
Before we could both get some sleep
He expected "Nothing to report sir"
So should our experience, we keep?

We thought we should give it a mention
To see how he would react
He eyed us both with suspicion
And told us we should use some tact

"No report of this nature is needed
It should not be mentioned again
You may both end up in the glass house
If you dare use a paper and pen"

I finished my time as a trooper
I came back to my civvy life
I worked hard and brought up a family
With the aid of my dear wife

I know what I saw, on that starry night
And although it was quite long ago
I am filled with an honest conviction
We had both seen a real UFO.

The Witch

The witch
on linen white she lay
in shuttered room
At end of day
her naked form
Stretched out and still
and thus she toiled
To work her will

She fasted
all the day before
She'd placed yon broomstick
at the door
To warn all callers
to beware
Disturb her not
nor challenge her

So quiet
and unearthly still
She set about
to work her will
Her body
slim and deathly white
It seemed to quiver
in the night

The quaking ceased
her breath
Stood still
her soul
Departed from its mill
arising quickly did ascend
A witch in flight
with tapered end

She rose in Astral
oh so high
She left the Earth
and wandered nigh
Into the void
she passed that way
There is no night
and is no day

For time
does not exist you see
Except to us
who humans be
In her ambitions
to arise
She clean forgot
her earthly ties

And now alone
the galax gone
And too afeared
to carry on
The panic welled
within her so
She did not know
which way to go

'Twas then
the Triangle on high
Came to her aid
as he passed by
A million leagues
of time depress
To help this maiden
in distress

He leant across the
frightened frame
And vowed to see her
home again
A corner wrapped
around her form
She felt the love
was true and warm

True love like this
she'd never felt before
She could not
see her saviour
But of her safety
she was sure
No movement felt
nor word was said

Then she awoke
in her own bed
For the love
new found
She longed once more
she'd search
And search
for ever more.

The Comforter

I wander around
the twilight zone
I have no place
to call my home
I am lost
to the infinity
I am human not
nor spirit be

I am the thought
within your head
I am the dream
you dream in bed
I am the answer
to your prayer
You turn to me
to ease your fear

A problem's answer
you may find
When I creep in and
open up your mind
I travel o'er
the Universe
I have no voice
so don't converse

In ways that
other forms may do
If you need me
I'll come to you
Just call for me
and I'll be there
You see I am
The Comforter.

Autumn Wind

The wind outside my window
as sleepless night I lay
Keeps talking of the old times
when I was young and gay

He speaks of friends we both knew well
for whom I feel forlorn
I wish that I could bring them back
forever they are gone

He calls me to the window
to watch him bend the tree
And moans about our gable
as he entreats with me

He calls me to the old times
and asks me to be free
And tempts me with the promise
of final liberty

I strongly feel the yearning
to cast this earthly form
To gander with him freely
and so forget it all

I hesitate and wonder
why he should entreat me
And now I know the answer
he's lonelier than me

For I am but a mortal
from cradle to the grave
He's lost more friends that I have
and he cannot renege

He's wandered Earth so freely
his duties to perform
Across the seas and mountains
since first the Holy dawn

He's seen the Titans come and go
the golden age of man
And whistled down the time zones
since first the world began

With Adam in the garden
with Neolithic man
He's seen the billions come and go
of time enslaving man

No wonder he is lonely
and mourns and sighs and so
For you and I can perish
but he's nowhere to go

You see, he is immortal
for him there is no end
He's got to keep on moving
and can't retain a friend

And so there is affection
twixt Autumn Wind and I
For he is just as badly off
because he cannot die.

A Focus Point

A star shone
In a distant place
With many facets
To its face

It is gazed upon
With love each night
Each person sees
A different sight

For each will see
The face they know
The face of one
That they loved so

They may look for
The brightest star
Or pick on one
That's not too far

But in this star
They're sure to find
The comfort to
Appease their mind

A place where they
Can silent be
While standing still
Let mind run free

When happy times
Come flooding in
To raise a smile
Perhaps a grin

A moment in
The sweet repose
Illuminated by
The star they chose

A focus point
They need you see
It represents
Eternity.

Love or Lust

When we seek a partner
We should respect the golden rule
To get to know each other
Not just dive in like a fool

If a person does not touch the soul
To cause at least, a little stir
Then we must ask the question
Whether love is really there

Or is it just emotion
That has stirred our sexual need
A feeling of high excitement
That must be cured with speed

Then when we put it to the test
If there is no depth at all
No substance for our love to grow
We know we're heading for a fall

Maundy Thursday

Where do we fit
    into this scheme
What are the dreams
    we dare to dream

Who are the actors
    in this play
The folk we meet
    along the way

Whose will, will take
    the leading role
Of on whose life
    the Bell will toll

Pontius Pilate's
    wrong decision
Left him with
    a haunting vision

Will Christ be waiting
    at that hour
Or Satan's call
    all souls devour

Will we become
    a child of light
Or darkness ever
    be our plight

Does our fate lie
    in our own hands
As we travel forth
    o'er foreign lands

Or is our destiny
    ordained
When we are born
    and we are named.

A Tramp

A tramp sat in
the market square
'though some folk wished
he was not there

They passed on by
with upturned nose
They did not like
his tattered clothes

They considered not
how he came to be
An outcast
in this society

They could only see
a downcast man
Begging with
an empty can

Then a passer by saying
"He's someone's son"
Handed him a drink
and a meat-filled bun

The tramp
accepted willingly
Saying "Thank you ma'am
for helping me

I lost my job
my home, my wife
I could not cope
with the pace of life

With money worries
to the fore
My so-called friends
showed me the door

They did not try
to understand
That I required
a helping hand

I trundled on
in dark despair
There was no one
to really care

No home, nor money
no food to eat
I took to begging
on the street

But begging is not
the life for me
This cannot be
my destiny

To sleep on benches
in the park
Afraid to close
my eyes when dark

To have no shelter
in the rain
When people fail
to hide distain

When cold and damp
head bowed with shame
A lonely tramp
without a name

For people don't ask
who you are
Nor question
"Have you travelled far?"

Some turn their head
and rush away
They cannot spare
the time of day

But now and then
a friendly face
Will help to lift
you up a pace

They let you know
that someone cares
And share with you
their food and wares

They help you find
a place to sleep
To wash and shower
and earn your keep

Then, if you're lucky
you may find
A pathway back
to Human kind"

The moral of
this story
If you don't
already know

That person sleeping
on the street
Has nowhere else
to go

So don't just
turn your head away
From that
awful man

Show a bit
of kindness
And help him
if you can.

The Portrait

There is a portrait
on the wall
Of a powerful man
both handsome and tall

Handsome and tall
and full of pride
There is also a horse
on which he'd ride

I wondered who
this man could be
Are we related
him and me?

In my mind's eye
I can recall
When I was young
and very small

This person came
and stayed for tea
I think he sat me
on his knee

My mother and
this man did chat
Of family things
of this and that

Of times before
I came to be
Of place still
unknown to me

Of happy times
when Mum was young
Of games they played
and songs they sung

But then Mum showed
him to the door
We never saw him
any more

And now I'm grown
and Mum has gone
So I am left
to ponder on

But I needn't
ponder any more
I found a letter
in the drawer

I read the letter
and had to laugh
There also was
a photograph

A photograph
of him and me
I was sitting
on his knee

'twas on that day
he stayed for tea
You see he is
my Grand-daddy.

Young Tramp

A tramp sat in
the Market place
A look of sadness
on his face

For times had changed
for this young lad
He'd lost his Mother
and his Dad

No family meant
for him no home
How could he manage
on his own

In the market place
he'd volunteer
Stall holders uttered
"no work here"

He would not steal
that's not his way
And so he hungered
all the day

And so he'd wait
"til day was done
And then he'd beg
for bread or bun.

Seven Candles

Seven candles burning
One for each new day
We've kept the candles burning
Ever since you went away.

Seven candles burning
Each one holds a prayer
Seven candles burning
With the hope that you can hear

Seven candles burning
Carrying our love
Seven candles burning
Their flames will rise above

Seven candles burning
One for each new day
We've kept the candles burning
Ever since you went away.

Reflection

I looked through the window
What did I see
Someone staring back
A reflection of me

I was laying in bed
It was in my mind's eye
The window was real
With folks passing by

I opened the window
And left it ajar
I could see through the gap
But not very far

My reflection reached through
And held out her hand
Come over to me
And explore my land

I accepted the challenge
Knowing not what I'd find
My reflection and me
Are two of a kind

It's a very strange feeling
To be facing yourself
My reflection is waiting
I proceed with stealth

I raise my right arm
But hers seems to be left
What would I find
As through the window I crept

Outside there's a pool
A child plays with a pup
I look down into the pool
But my reflection looks up

My eyes scout around
Surveying the track
I take a step forward
My reflection steps back

Wherever you go
Your reflection goes too
And just like your shadow
Is an image of you.

Vicar Vicar

"Oh Vicar, Vicar
Bless me please
For surely I have sinned"

"Then tell me boy"
The Vicar said
With lips pierced tight and thinned

"What is this deed
That you have done
To make you think you've sinned"

A little voice
Was heard to say
"I peed against the wind".